IRISH
COOKING BIBLE

More than 120 delicious recipes from
pub fare to country classics

Publications International, Ltd.

Photography on pages 7, 11, 15, 19, 23, 27, 35, 39, 41, 43, 47, 49, 51, 55, 57, 65, 67, 69, 71, 79, 81, 87, 91, 101, 103, 105, 107, 109, 111, 113, 115, 117, 119, 121, 123, 125, 127, 129, 137, 143, 145, 147, 149, 155, 157, 161, 167, 173, 179 and 183 by PIL Photo Studio North.

Recipe development on pages 6, 10, 40, 42, 46, 48, 50, 54, 64, 68, 102, 104, 108, 110, 112, 116, 118, 120, 128, 144, 146, 148, 166 and 178 by David Bonom.
Recipe development on pages 22, 56, 66, 78, 80, 86, 90, 114, 124, 136, 142, 154, 156, 160, 172 and 182 by Marilyn Pocius.
Recipe development on pages 14, 18, 26, 34, 38, 70, 100, 106, 122 and 126 by Sandra Wu.

Pictured on the front cover: Pub-Style Fish and Chips *(page 130)*.
Pictured on the back cover *(clockwise from top left)*: Chicken, Barley and Vegetable Soup *(page 24)*, Corned Beef and Cabbage with Horseradish Mustard Sauce *(page 62)* and Irish Soda Bread *(page 150)*.

ISBN-13: 978-1-4508-6840-2
ISBN-10: 1-4508-6840-1

Library of Congress Control Number: 2013933614

Manufactured in China.

8 7 6 5 4 3 2 1

Publications International, Ltd.

CONTENTS

Raisin Oat Scones

2 cups all-purpose flour
2 teaspoons baking powder
½ teaspoon baking soda
¼ teaspoon salt
1 cup old-fashioned oats
½ cup (1 stick) cold butter, cut into pieces
1 cup raisins
1 cup buttermilk

1. Preheat oven to 425°F. Grease baking sheets.

2. Sift flour, baking powder, baking soda and salt into medium bowl. Stir in oats. Cut in butter with pastry blender or two knives until mixture resembles coarse crumbs. Stir in raisins. Stir in just enough buttermilk to make soft dough.

3. Turn out dough onto lightly floured surface; knead several times until smooth. Pat dough into 12×10-inch rectangle. Cut into 2-inch squares; arrange on prepared baking sheets.

4. Bake about 15 minutes or until browned. Remove to wire rack to cool slightly.

Makes 30 scones

Irish Whiskey Cured Salmon

1 skin-on salmon fillet (1¾ pounds), pin bones removed
2 tablespoons Irish whiskey
⅓ cup packed dark brown sugar
3 tablespoons salt
    Black bread or Irish soda bread (optional)
    Crème fraîche, thinly sliced red onion and/or capers (optional)

1. Line rimmed baking sheet with plastic wrap. Rinse salmon and pat dry with paper towels. Arrange salmon, skin side down, on prepared baking sheet; brush salmon flesh with whiskey.

2. Combine brown sugar and salt in small bowl; rub mixture all over salmon flesh. Wrap plastic wrap securely around salmon. Top with another sheet of plastic wrap.

3. Place second baking sheet on top of salmon, then place heavy skillet or several cans on top to weigh it down. Refrigerate salmon at least 48 hours and up to 72 hours.

4. Remove top baking sheet. Unwrap salmon and rinse under cold water to remove any salt mixture that remains. Pat dry with paper towels. Cut salmon into very thin slices; serve with bread and assorted toppings, if desired. Refrigerate leftover salmon up to 2 days.

Makes 6 to 8 servings

TIP Ask your fishmonger to remove the pin bones when purchasing the salmon. (Often this is already done, or you can remove the pin bones at home with tweezers.)

Hot Cross Buns

1 package (¼ ounce) active dry yeast
1 cup warm milk, divided
2¼ cups all-purpose flour
1 cup currants
½ cup whole wheat flour
¼ cup granulated sugar
¼ teaspoon salt
¼ teaspoon ground nutmeg
2 eggs, beaten
¼ cup (½ stick) butter, melted
½ cup powdered sugar
1 to 2 tablespoons milk or cream

1. Sprinkle yeast over ¼ cup warm milk in small bowl; stir to dissolve yeast. Let stand 10 minutes or until bubbly. Meanwhile, combine all-purpose flour, currants, whole wheat flour, granulated sugar, salt and nutmeg in medium bowl. Whisk eggs, butter and remaining ¾ cup warm milk in large bowl.

2. Stir dissolved yeast into egg mixture. Gradually beat in flour mixture until well blended. (Dough will be sticky.) Cover and let rise in warm place 1 hour.

3. Preheat oven to 400°F. Grease 12 standard (2½-inch) muffin cups. Vigorously stir down dough with wooden spoon. Spoon about ¼ cup dough into each muffin cup; smooth tops.

4. Bake 20 minutes or until golden brown. Cool buns in pan 5 minutes; remove to wire rack to cool completely.

5. Whisk powdered sugar and milk in small bowl until smooth. Spoon icing into small resealable food storage bag. Cut off small corner of bag; pipe cross on center of each bun.

Makes 12 buns

Irish Porridge with Berry Compote

4 cups plus 1 tablespoon water, divided
½ teaspoon salt
1 cup steel-cut oats
½ teaspoon ground cinnamon
⅓ cup half-and-half
¼ cup packed brown sugar
1 cup fresh strawberries, hulled and quartered
1 container (6 ounces) fresh blackberries
1 container (6 ounces) fresh blueberries
3 tablespoons granulated sugar

1. Bring 4 cups water and salt to a boil in medium saucepan over medium-high heat. Whisk in oats and cinnamon; simmer, uncovered, over medium heat about 40 minutes or until water is absorbed and oats are tender. Remove from heat; stir in half-and-half and brown sugar. Keep warm.

2. Meanwhile, combine strawberries, blackberries, blueberries, granulated sugar and remaining 1 tablespon water in small saucepan; bring to a simmer over medium heat. Cook 8 to 9 minutes or until berries are tender but still hold their shape, stirring occasionally. Divide porridge among four bowls; top with berry compote.

Makes 4 servings

Date-Nut Granola

2 cups old-fashioned oats
2 cups barley flakes
1 cup sliced almonds
⅓ cup vegetable oil
⅓ cup honey
1 teaspoon vanilla
1 cup chopped dates

1. Preheat oven to 350°F. Grease 13×9-inch baking pan. Combine oats, barley flakes and almonds in large bowl. Combine oil, honey and vanilla in small bowl. Pour honey mixture over oat mixture; mix well to coat. Pour into prepared pan.

2. Bake about 25 minutes or until toasted, stirring frequently after first 10 minutes. Stir in dates while granola is still hot. Cool. Store tightly covered. *Makes 6 cups*

Irish Porridge with Berry Compote

Caramelized Bacon

12 slices (about 12 ounces) applewood-smoked bacon
½ cup packed brown sugar
2 tablespoons water
¼ to ½ teaspoon ground red pepper

1. Preheat oven to 375°F. Line 15×10-inch jelly-roll pan with heavy-duty foil. Spray wire rack with nonstick cooking spray; place in prepared pan.

2. Cut bacon in half crosswise, if desired; arrange in single layer on prepared wire rack. Combine brown sugar, water and red pepper in small bowl; mix well. Brush generously over bacon.

3. Bake 20 to 25 minutes or until bacon is well browned. Immediately transfer to serving platter; cool completely. *Makes 6 servings*

Baked Oatmeal

1 cup old-fashioned oats
1 teaspoon ground cinnamon, divided
¼ teaspoon salt
1½ cups milk
1 egg
2 tablespoons honey
1 tablespoon butter, melted
1 teaspoon vanilla
1 cup chopped peeled apple
3 tablespoons finely chopped dried fruit
¼ cup chopped nuts (optional)

1. Preheat oven to 350°F. Spray 1½- to 2-quart baking dish with nonstick cooking spray.

2. Combine oats, ½ teaspoon cinnamon and salt in large bowl. Combine milk, egg, honey, butter and vanilla in medium bowl; stir into oat mixture. Stir in apple and dried fruit. Pour mixture into prepared baking dish; sprinkle with remaining ½ teaspoon cinnamon.

3. Bake 40 to 45 minutes or until knife inserted into center comes out clean. Let stand 5 minutes before serving. Sprinkle with nuts, if desired. *Makes 4 servings*

Smoked Salmon and Spinach Frittata

2 tablespoons vegetable oil, divided
1 medium red onion, diced
1 clove garlic, minced
6 ounces baby spinach
10 eggs
1 teaspoon dried dill weed
¼ teaspoon salt
¼ teaspoon black pepper
4 ounces smoked salmon, chopped
4 ounces Dubliner cheese, cut into ¼-inch cubes

1. Position oven rack in upper-middle position. Preheat broiler.

2. Heat 1 tablespoon oil in large ovenproof nonstick skillet. Add onion; cook 7 to 8 minutes or until softened, stirring occasionally. Add garlic; cook and stir 1 minute. Add spinach; cook and stir 3 minutes or until just wilted. Transfer mixture to small bowl.

3. Whisk eggs, dill, salt and pepper in large bowl until blended. Stir in salmon, cheese and spinach mixture.

4. Heat remaining 1 tablespoon oil in same skillet over medium heat. Add egg mixture; cook about 3 minutes, stirring gently to form large curds. Cook undisturbed 5 minutes or until eggs are just beginning to set.

5. Transfer skillet to oven. Broil 2 to 3 minutes or until frittata is puffed, set and lightly browned. Let stand 5 minutes; carefully slide frittata onto large plate or cutting board. Cut into wedges.   *Makes 6 to 8 servings*

Corned Beef Hash

2 large russet potatoes, peeled and cut into ½-inch cubes
½ teaspoon salt
¼ teaspoon black pepper
¼ cup (½ stick) butter
1 cup chopped onion
½ pound corned beef, finely chopped
1 tablespoon horseradish
4 eggs

1. Place potatoes in large skillet; add cold water to cover. Bring to a boil over high heat. Reduce heat to low; simmer 6 minutes. (Potatoes will be firm.) Remove potatoes from skillet; drain well. Sprinkle with salt and pepper.

2. Melt butter in same skillet over medium heat. Add onion; cook and stir 5 minutes. Stir in corned beef, horseradish and potatoes; mix well. Press mixture with spatula to flatten.

3. Reduce heat to low; cook 10 to 15 minutes. Turn hash in large pieces; pat down and cook 10 to 15 minutes or until bottom is well browned.

4. Meanwhile, bring 1 inch of water to a simmer in small saucepan. Break 1 egg into shallow dish; carefully slide into water. Cook 5 minutes or until white is opaque. Remove with slotted spoon to plate; keep warm. Repeat with remaining eggs.

5. Top each serving of hash with 1 egg. Serve immediately.   *Makes 4 servings*

Bacon and Potato Quiche

   1 refrigerated pie crust (half of 15-ounce package)
12 ounces thick-cut bacon, cut crosswise into ½-inch pieces
   ½ medium onion, chopped
   8 ounces Yukon Gold potatoes, peeled and cut into ¼-inch cubes
   ½ teaspoon chopped fresh thyme leaves
1½ cups half-and-half
   4 eggs
   ½ teaspoon salt
   ½ teaspoon black pepper
   ¾ cup (3 ounces) shredded Dubliner cheese
   2 tablespoons chopped fresh chives

1. Preheat oven to 450°F. Line baking sheet with foil.

2. Roll out pie crust into 12-inch circle on floured surface. Line 9-inch glass pie plate with crust, pressing firmly against bottom and up side of plate. Trim crust to leave 1-inch overhang; fold under and flute edge. Prick bottom of crust with fork. Bake about 8 minutes or until crust is lightly browned. Transfer to wire rack to cool slightly. *Reduce oven temperature to 375°F.*

3. Cook bacon in large skillet over medium heat about 10 minutes or until crisp, stirring occasionally. Drain bacon on paper towel-lined plate. Drain all but 1 tablespoon drippings from skillet. Add onion, potatoes and thyme to skillet; cook about 10 minutes or until onion and potatoes are tender, stirring occasionally.

4. Place pie plate on prepared baking sheet. Whisk half-and-half, eggs, salt and pepper in medium until well blended. Sprinkle cheese evenly over bottom of crust; top with onion mixture. Pour in egg mixture; sprinkle with chives.

5. Bake 35 to 40 minutes or until quiche is set and knife inserted into center comes out clean. Cool 10 minutes before slicing.   *Makes 8 servings*

Oxtail Soup

2½ pounds oxtails (beef or veal)
1 large onion, sliced
4 carrots, cut into 1-inch pieces, divided
3 stalks celery, cut into 1-inch pieces, divided
2 sprigs fresh parsley
5 whole black peppercorns
1 bay leaf
4 cups beef broth
1 cup dark beer
2 cups diced baking potatoes
1 teaspoon salt
2 tablespoons chopped fresh parsley (optional)

1. Combine oxtails, onion, half of carrots, one third of celery, parsley, peppercorns and bay leaf in large saucepan or Dutch oven. Add broth and beer; bring to a boil over medium-high heat. Reduce heat to low; cover and simmer 3 hours or until meat is falling off bones.

2. Remove oxtails and set aside. Strain broth and return to saucepan; skim fat. Add remaining carrots, celery and potatoes; bring to a simmer. Cook 10 to 15 minutes or until vegetables are tender.

3. Remove meat from oxtails; discard bones. Stir meat and salt into soup; cook until heated through. Sprinkle with chopped parsley, if desired. *Makes 4 servings*

Cock-A-Leekie Soup

4 cups reduced-sodium chicken broth
4 cups water
2½ pounds chicken thighs (with bones and skin)
3 stalks celery, sliced
2 bay leaves
5 to 6 large leeks (about 2½ pounds)
½ cup uncooked pearl barley
1 teaspoon salt
1 teaspoon ground allspice
12 pitted prunes, halved
   Additional salt and black pepper

1. Combine broth, water, chicken, celery and bay leaves in large saucepan or Dutch oven; bring to a boil over high heat. Reduce heat to low; cover and simmer 30 minutes or until chicken is tender. Remove chicken to cutting board to cool.

2. Meanwhile, trim leeks. Cut off roots, any damaged leaves and very tough tops. Cut in half lengthwise, then cut crosswise into ¾-inch pieces. Wash well in several changes of water.

3. Add leeks, barley, salt and allspice to saucepan; cover and simmer 40 minutes or until leeks and barley are tender.

4. Remove skin and bones from chicken; cut into bite-size pieces. Add to soup with prunes; simmer 3 minutes or until prunes soften. Season with salt and pepper.

Makes 6 to 8 servings

Chicken, Barley and Vegetable Soup

½ pound boneless skinless chicken breasts, cut into ½-inch pieces
½ pound boneless skinless chicken thighs, cut into ½-inch pieces
1 teaspoon salt
¼ teaspoon black pepper
1 tablespoon olive oil
½ cup uncooked pearl barley
4 cans (about 14 ounces each) reduced-sodium chicken broth
2 cups water
1 bay leaf
2 cups whole baby carrots
2 cups diced peeled potatoes
2 cups sliced mushrooms
2 cup frozen peas
3 tablespoons sour cream
1 tablespoon chopped fresh dill *or* 1 teaspoon dried dill weed

1. Sprinkle chicken with salt and pepper. Heat oil in large saucepan or Dutch oven over medium-high heat. Add chicken; cook without stirring 2 minutes or until golden. Turn chicken; cook 2 minutes. Remove chicken to plate.

2. Add barley to saucepan; cook and stir 1 to 2 minutes or until barley begins to brown, adding 1 tablespoon broth if needed to prevent burning. Add remaining broth, water and bay leaf; bring to a boil. Reduce heat to low; cover and simmer 30 minutes.

3. Add chicken, carrots, potatoes and mushrooms; cook 10 minutes or until vegetables are tender. Add peas; cook 2 minutes. Remove and discard bay leaf.

4. Top with sour cream and dill; serve immediately.   *Makes 6 servings*

Cod Chowder

2 tablespoons vegetable oil
1 pound red potatoes, diced
2 medium leeks, halved and thinly sliced
2 stalks celery, diced
1 bulb fennel, diced
½ yellow or red bell pepper, diced
2 teaspoons chopped fresh thyme
¾ teaspoon salt
½ to ¾ teaspoon black pepper
2 tablespoons all-purpose flour
2 cups clam juice
1 cup water
1 cup half-and-half
1 cup frozen corn
1½ pounds cod, cut into 1-inch pieces
¼ cup finely chopped fresh Italian parsley

1. Heat oil in Dutch oven or large saucepan over medium heat. Add potatoes, leeks, celery, fennel, bell pepper, thyme, salt and pepper; cover and cook about 8 minutes or until vegetables are slightly softened, stirring occasionally. Add flour; cook and stir 1 minute.

2. Stir in clam juice and water; bring to a boil over high heat. Reduce heat to medium-low; cover and simmer about 10 minutes or until potatoes are tender. Remove from heat.

3. Transfer 1½ cups soup to blender; add half-and-half and blend until smooth.

4. Add corn, cod and parsley to saucepan; bring to a simmer over medium-high heat. Stir in blended soup mixture; cover and cook over medium heat about 3 minutes or until fish is firm and opaque, stirring occasionally. Serve immediately.

Makes 6 to 8 servings

Pork and Cabbage Soup

½ pound pork loin, cut into ½-inch cubes
1 medium onion, chopped
2 slices bacon, finely chopped
2 cups reduced-sodium beef broth
2 cups reduced-sodium chicken broth
1 can (about 28 ounces) whole tomatoes, drained and coarsely chopped
2 medium carrots, sliced
¾ teaspoon dried marjoram
1 bay leaf
⅛ teaspoon black pepper
¼ medium cabbage, chopped
2 tablespoons chopped fresh parsley

1. Heat large saucepan or Dutch oven over medium heat. Add pork, onion and bacon; cook and stir until meat is no longer pink and onion is crisp-tender. Drain fat.

2. Stir in broth, tomatoes, carrots, marjoram, bay leaf and pepper; bring to a boil over high heat. Reduce heat to medium-low; simmer, uncovered, about 30 minutes. Remove and discard bay leaf. Skim off fat.

3. Add cabbage; bring to a boil over high heat. Reduce heat to medium-low; simmer, uncovered, about 15 minutes or until cabbage is tender. Stir in parsley.

Makes 6 servings

TIP Bacon is much easier to chop when it is partially frozen, but it can be difficult to separate the slices. For easier separation, roll up the package before you open it, then unroll and flatten it out—single strips can then easily be peeled off without sticking. Once the package is opened, the remaining bacon should be tightly wrapped and stored in the refrigerator for up to 1 week.

Double Pea Soup

1 tablespoon vegetable oil
1 onion, finely chopped
3 cloves garlic, minced
4 cups water
2 cups dried split peas
1 bay leaf
1 teaspoon ground mustard
1½ cups frozen green peas
1 teaspoon salt
¼ teaspoon black pepper
   Sour cream

1. Heat oil in large saucepan or Dutch oven over medium-high heat. Add onion; cook 5 minutes or until tender, stirring occasionally. Add garlic; cook and stir 1 minute.

2. Add water, split peas, bay leaf and mustard; bring to a boil over high heat. Reduce heat to medium-low; cover and simmer 45 minutes or until split peas are tender, stirring occasionally.

3. Stir in green peas, salt and pepper; cover and simmer 10 minutes or until green peas are tender. Remove and discard bay leaf. Working in batches, purée soup in blender or food processor until smooth.

4. Top each serving with sour cream.   *Makes 6 servings*

Beef Barley Soup

1 tablespoon vegetable oil
¾ pound boneless beef top round steak, trimmed and cut into ½-inch pieces
3 cans (about 14 ounces each) reduced-sodium beef broth
2 cups unpeeled cubed potatoes
1 can (about 14 ounces) diced tomatoes
1 cup chopped onion
1 cup sliced carrots
½ cup uncooked pearl barley
1 tablespoon cider vinegar
2 teaspoons caraway seeds
2 teaspoons dried marjoram
2 teaspoons dried thyme
½ teaspoon salt
½ teaspoon black pepper
1½ cups sliced green beans (½-inch slices)

1. Heat oil in large saucepan or Dutch oven over medium heat. Add beef; cook and stir until browned on all sides.

2. Stir in broth, potatoes, tomatoes, onion, carrots, barley, vinegar, caraway seeds, marjoram, thyme, salt and pepper; bring to a boil over high heat. Reduce heat to low; cover and simmer 1½ hours. Add green beans; cook, uncovered, 30 minutes or until beef is fork-tender.   *Makes 4 servings*

Curried Parsnip Soup

3 pounds parsnips, peeled and cut into 2-inch pieces
1 tablespoon olive oil
2 tablespoons butter
1 medium yellow onion, chopped
2 stalks celery, diced
3 cloves garlic, minced
1 tablespoon salt
1 to 2 teaspoons curry powder
½ teaspoon grated fresh ginger
½ teaspoon black pepper
8 cups reduced-sodium chicken broth
   Toasted bread slices (optional)
   Chopped fresh chives (optional)

1. Preheat oven to 400°F. Line large baking sheet with foil.

2. Combine parsnips and oil in large bowl; toss to coat. Spread in single layer on prepared baking sheet. Bake 35 to 45 minutes or until parsnips are tender and lightly browned around edges, stirring once halfway through cooking.

3. Melt butter in large saucepan or Dutch oven over medium heat. Add onion and celery; cook about 8 minutes or until tender and onion is translucent. Add garlic, salt, curry powder, ginger and pepper; cook and stir 1 minute. Add parsnips and broth; bring to a simmer over medium-high heat. Reduce heat to medium-low; cover and cook 10 minutes.

4. Working in batches, purée soup in blender or food processor. Transfer blended soup to large heatproof bowl. Garnish with toasted bread and chives.   *Makes 6 to 8 servings*

Mulligatawny Soup

1 tablespoon olive oil
1 pound boneless skinless chicken breasts, cut into ½-inch pieces
2 cups finely chopped carrots
1 cup chopped green bell pepper
2 stalks celery, thinly sliced
½ cup finely chopped onion
3 cloves garlic, minced
¼ cup all-purpose flour
1 to 2 teaspoons curry powder
¼ teaspoon ground nutmeg
3 cups reduced-sodium chicken broth
1 cup milk
1 cup chopped seeded tomato
1 medium apple, peeled and sliced
¼ cup uncooked converted rice
½ teaspoon salt
⅛ teaspoon black pepper

1. Heat oil in large saucepan or Dutch oven over medium heat. Add chicken, carrots, bell pepper, celery, onion and garlic; cook and stir 5 minutes. Sprinkle with flour, curry powder and nutmeg; cook and stir 1 to 2 minutes.

2. Add broth, milk, tomato, apple, rice, salt and black pepper; bring to a boil. Reduce heat to low; cover and simmer 20 minutes or until rice is tender.   *Makes 8 servings*

Pan-Seared Sole with Lemon-Butter Caper Sauce

¼ cup all-purpose flour
½ teaspoon plus ⅛ teaspoon salt, divided
¼ teaspoon black pepper
1 pound Dover sole fillets
2 tablespoons vegetable oil
3 tablespoons butter
2 tablespoons lemon juice
2 teaspoons capers, rinsed, drained and chopped
2 tablespoons finely chopped fresh chives

1. Whisk flour, ½ teaspoon salt and pepper in pie plate or shallow dish. Coat fillets with flour mixture, shaking off excess.

2. Heat oil in large nonstick skillet over medium heat. Add half of fillets; cook 2 to 3 minutes per side or until golden brown. Transfer to plate and tent with foil to keep warm. Repeat with remaining fillets.

3. Wipe out skillet with paper towels. Add butter and remaining ⅛ teaspoon salt; cook 20 to 30 seconds or until melted and lightly browned. Remove from heat; stir in lemon juice and capers.

4. Drizzle sauce over fish; sprinkle with chives. Serve immediately.   *Makes 2 servings*

Traditional Mussels in Cream

2 tablespoons butter
1 medium onion, chopped
4 cloves garlic, minced
1 sprig fresh thyme
1 bay leaf
¾ cup whipping cream
¼ teaspoon salt
2 pounds mussels, scrubbed and debearded
1 tablespoon lemon juice
    Crusty bread for serving

1. Melt butter in large saucepan over medium-high heat. Add onion and garlic; cook about 2 minutes or until garlic starts to brown slightly. Add thyme and bay leaf; cook 30 seconds. Add cream and salt; bring to a boil and cook 1 minute.

2. Add mussels to saucepan; cover and bring to a boil. Cook 4 to 5 minutes or until mussels open. Uncover saucepan; cook 1 minute. Remove from heat; stir in lemon juice. Discard any unopened mussels. Serve immediately in bowls with bread.

Makes 4 appetizer servings

Dill-Crusted Salmon

4 salmon fillets (about 5 ounces each)
½ cup panko bread crumbs
½ cup finely chopped fresh dill
3 tablespoons mayonnaise
2 tablespoons olive oil
1 teaspoon salt
½ teaspoon red pepper flakes

1. Preheat oven to 400°F. Spray rack in roasting pan with nonstick cooking spray. Place salmon on rack.

2. Combine panko, dill, mayonnaise, oil, salt and red pepper flakes in medium bowl; mix well. Mound mixture evenly on top of fillets, pressing to adhere.

3. Bake 20 to 25 minutes or until topping is browned and fish just begins to flake when tested with fork.

Makes 4 servings

Pan-Fried Oysters

¼ cup all-purpose flour
½ teaspoon salt
¼ teaspoon black pepper
2 eggs
½ cup plain dry bread crumbs
5 tablespoons chopped fresh parsley, divided
2 containers (8 ounces each) shucked fresh oysters, rinsed, drained and patted dry
   or 1 pound fresh oysters, shucked and patted dry
   Canola oil for frying
5 slices Irish bacon, crisp-cooked and chopped
   Lemon wedges

1. Combine flour, salt and pepper in pie plate or shallow dish. Beat eggs in shallow bowl. Combine bread crumbs and 4 tablespoons parsley in second bowl.

2. Working with one oyster at a time, coat with flour mixture, shaking off excess. Dip in eggs, shaking off excess; roll in bread crumb mixture to coat.

3. Heat ½ inch oil in large skillet over medium-high heat until very hot but not smoking (about 370°F). Add one third of oysters; cook about 2 minutes per side or until golden brown. Drain on paper towel-lined plate. Repeat with remaining oysters.

4. Toss oysters with bacon and remaining 1 tablespoon parsley in large bowl. Serve immediately with lemon wedges.   *Makes 4 appetizer servings*

Roasted Dill Scrod with Asparagus

1 bunch (12 ounces) asparagus spears, ends trimmed
1 tablespoon olive oil
4 scrod or cod fish fillets (about 5 ounces each)
1 tablespoon lemon juice
1 teaspoon dried dill weed
½ teaspoon salt
¼ teaspoon black pepper
Paprika (optional)

1. Preheat oven to 425°F.

2. Place asparagus in 13×9-inch baking dish; drizzle with oil. Roll asparagus to coat lightly with oil; push to edges of dish, stacking asparagus into two layers.

3. Arrange fish fillets in center of dish; drizzle with lemon juice. Combine dill, salt and pepper in small bowl; sprinkle over fish and asparagus.

4. Roast 15 to 17 minutes or until asparagus is crisp-tender and fish is opaque in center and just begins to flake when tested with fork. *Makes 4 servings*

Salmon Patties

1 can (12 ounces) pink salmon, undrained
1 egg, lightly beaten
¼ cup minced green onions
1 tablespoon chopped fresh dill
1 clove garlic, minced
½ cup all-purpose flour
1½ teaspoons baking powder
1½ cups vegetable oil

1. Drain salmon, reserving 2 tablespoons liquid. Place salmon in medium bowl; break apart with fork. Add reserved liquid, egg, green onions, dill and garlic; mix well.

2. Combine flour and baking powder in small bowl; add to salmon mixture. Stir until well blended. Shape mixture into six patties.

3. Heat oil in large skillet to 350°F. Add patties; cook until golden brown on both sides. Drain on paper towel-lined plate. Serve warm. *Makes 6 patties*

Pan-Seared Scallops with Mushrooms and Leeks

  3 tablespoons butter, divided
1½ pounds sea scallops, patted dry
  ½ teaspoon salt, divided
  ¼ teaspoon black pepper, divided
  1 package (8 ounces) sliced white mushrooms
  3 medium leeks, white and light green parts only, cut in half crosswise
      and very thinly sliced lengthwise
  2 cloves garlic, minced
  ½ cup vermouth or dry white wine
  ⅓ cup whipping cream
  ¼ cup (1 ounce) shredded Dubliner cheese

1. Melt 1 tablespoon butter in large nonstick skillet over medium-high heat. Sprinkle scallops with ¼ teaspoon salt and ⅛ teaspoon pepper. Add to skillet; cook 2 to 3 minutes per side or until browned and opaque. (Cook in batches if necessary to prevent overcrowding.) Transfer scallops to plate; keep warm.

2. Melt remaining 2 tablespoons butter in skillet over medium-high heat. Add mushrooms; cook 3 to 4 minutes or until mushrooms just start to brown slightly. Stir in leeks and garlic; cook and stir 3 to 4 minutes or until leeks are tender. Add vermouth; cook 1 to 2 minutes or until almost evaporated. Stir in cream; bring to a boil and cook about 1 minute. Stir in cheese, remaining ¼ teaspoon salt and ⅛ teaspoon pepper; cook and stir about 30 seconds or until cheese melts.

3. Return scallops to skillet; cook 1 to 2 minutes or until heated through. Serve immediately.   *Makes 4 servings*

Roasted Salmon Fillets with Irish Whiskey Sauce

4 salmon fillets (about 6 ounces each)
½ teaspoon salt, divided
⅛ teaspoon black pepper
⅓ cup Irish whiskey
¼ cup finely chopped shallots
1 tablespoon white wine vinegar
½ cup whipping cream
1½ teaspoons Dijon mustard
2 tablespoons butter, cut into small pieces
2 tablespoons chopped fresh chives

1. Position rack in center of oven. Preheat oven to 425°F. Spray rimmed baking sheet with nonstick cooking spray.

2. Sprinkle salmon fillets with ¼ teaspoon salt and pepper; arrange on prepared baking sheet. Roast salmon 8 to 10 minutes or until fish just begins to flake when tested with fork.

3. Meanwhile, combine whiskey, shallots and vinegar in small saucepan; bring to a boil over medium-high heat. Cook about 4 minutes or until liquid nearly evaporates and mixture looks like wet sand. Stir in cream and mustard; cook and stir 2 minutes or until slightly thickened. Remove from heat; whisk in butter, chives and remaining ¼ teaspoon salt.

4. Spoon sauce over salmon. Serve immediately.

Makes 4 servings

Simple Baked Cod

4 cod fillets (about 6 ounces each)
½ teaspoon salt
¼ teaspoon black pepper
¼ cup (½ stick) butter
1 teaspoon chopped fresh thyme
2 teaspoons grated lemon peel
3 tablespoons chopped fresh parsley

1. Position rack in center of oven. Preheat oven to 425°F. Spray rimmed baking sheet with nonstick cooking spray.

2. Sprinkle cod fillets with salt and pepper; arrange on prepared baking sheet. Bake 12 to 14 minutes or until fish just begins to flake when tested with fork.

3. Melt butter in small saucepan over medium heat. Stir in thyme and lemon peel; cook 1 minute. Remove from heat; stir in parsley. Spoon butter mixture over cod. Serve immediately.   *Makes 4 servings*

Oyster Chowder

4 slices thick-cut bacon, diced
1¼ cups chopped onion
1 can (about 14 ounces) chicken or vegetable broth
1¼ cups diced peeled potato
1 pint fresh shucked oysters, drained and liquor reserved
1 cup whipping cream or half-and-half
Salt and black pepper
Sliced green onions (optional)

1. Cook bacon in large saucepan over medium heat until crisp, stirring frequently. Drain on paper towel-lined plate.

2. Drain all but about 2 tablespoons drippings from skillet. Add onion to skillet; cook and stir 5 minutes or until tender. Add broth, potato and oyster liquor; cover and cook over medium-high heat 5 minutes or until potato is tender but firm. Stir in oysters and cream; cook 5 minutes or until edges of oysters begin to curl.

3. Season with salt and pepper. Ladle into bowls; top with bacon and green onions, if desired.   *Makes 4 servings*

Broiled Tilapia with Mustard Cream Sauce

4 fresh or thawed frozen tilapia fillets (about ¾ inch thick and 4 ounces each)
  Black pepper
½ cup sour cream
2 tablespoons chopped fresh dill
4 teaspoons Dijon mustard
2 teaspoons lemon juice
⅛ teaspoon garlic powder

1. Preheat broiler. Lightly spray rack of broiler pan with nonstick cooking spray.

2. Place fish on rack; sprinkle with pepper. Broil 4 to 5 inches from heat 5 to 8 minutes or until fish just begins to flake when tested with fork.

3. Meanwhile, combine sour cream, dill, mustard, lemon juice and garlic powder in small bowl. Serve over warm fish.   *Makes 4 servings*

TIP When purchasing fresh fish, make sure the fillets have a moist appearance, firm texture and a mild, fresh odor. (They should not smell fishy.) When purchasing raw frozen fish, make sure the fillets are completely frozen; there should be no dark, white or dry spots that might indicate the firsh has been thawed and refrozen. Frozen fish can be stored in the freezer for up to 6 months.

Pan-Roasted Pike with Buttery Bread Crumbs

6 tablespoons butter, divided
2 cloves garlic, minced
⅓ cup plain dry bread crumbs
½ teaspoon salt, divided
¼ cup chopped fresh parsley
4 pike fillets or other medium-firm white fish (about 6 ounces each)
⅛ teaspoon black pepper
2 tablespoons lemon juice

1. Preheat oven to 400°F.

2. Melt 2 tablespoons butter in small nonstick skillet over medium-high heat. Add garlic; cook and stir 1 minute or until lightly browned. Stir in bread crumbs and ⅛ teaspoon salt; cook and stir 1 minute. Transfer to small bowl; stir in parsley.

3. Melt 1 tablespoon butter in large ovenproof nonstick skillet over medium-high heat. Sprinkle pike fillets with ¼ teaspoon salt and pepper. Add to skillet, flesh side down; cook 1 minute. Remove from heat; turn fish and top with bread crumb mixture. Transfer to oven; roast 8 to 10 minutes or until fish just begins to flake when tested with fork.

4. Wipe out small skillet with paper towel; heat over medium heat. Add remaining 3 tablespoons butter; cook 3 to 4 minutes or until melted and lightly browned, stirring occasionally. Stir in lemon juice and remaining ⅛ teaspoon salt. Spoon mixture over fish just before serving.

Makes 4 servings

Trout with Mushrooms and Potato-Parsnip Mash

4 medium potatoes, peeled and cut into chunks
4 medium parsnips, peeled and cut into chunks
¼ cup all-purpose flour
½ teaspoon dried thyme
¼ teaspoon salt
¼ teaspoon black pepper
2 fresh whole trout (about 12 ounces each), filleted
¼ cup (½ stick) butter, divided
12 ounces cremini mushrooms, sliced
¼ cup dry white or rosé wine
1 tablespoon minced fresh sage

1. Place potatoes and parsnips in large saucepan; add cold water to cover. Bring to a boil over high heat. Reduce heat to medium-low; simmer until vegetables are fork-tender.

2. Meanwhile, combine flour, thyme, salt and pepper in shallow dish. Coat trout fillets with flour mixture, shaking off excess. Heat 2 tablespoons butter in large skillet over medium-high heat. Add fish to skillet in single layer; cook 1 to 2 minutes per side until fish just begins to flake when tested with fork. Remove from skillet and keep warm.

3. Add mushrooms to skillet; cook and stir 3 minutes, adding additional butter if needed to prevent scorching. Season with salt and pepper. Add wine; cook and stir until most of liquid has evaporated.

4. Drain potatoes and parsnips; return to saucepan and mash. Stir in remaining 2 tablespoons butter and sage; season with salt and pepper. Serve trout over mashed vegetables; top with mushrooms.   *Makes 4 servings*

Spicy Ale Shrimp

Dipping Sauce (recipe follows)
3 bottles (12 ounces each) pilsner beer, divided
1 tablespoon seafood boil seasoning blend
1 teaspoon mustard seeds
1 teaspoon red pepper flakes
2 lemons, quartered, divided
1 pound large raw shrimp, peeled and deveined (with tails on)

1. Prepare Dipping Sauce; set aside. Pour 1 bottle of beer into large bowl half filled with ice; set aside.

2. Fill large saucepan half full with water. Add remaining 2 bottles of beer, seafood seasoning, mustard seeds and red pepper flakes. Squeeze 4 lemon quarters into saucepan and add lemon quarters. Bring to a boil over medium-high heat.

3. Add shrimp to saucepan; cover and remove from heat. Let stand 3 minutes or until shrimp are pink and opaque. Drain shrimp; transfer to bowl of chilled beer and ice. Cool. Remove shrimp from bowl; arrange on platter. Serve with Dipping Sauce and remaining lemon quarters. *Makes 15 to 20 shrimp*

Dipping Sauce

1 cup ketchup
1 tablespoon chili-garlic paste
1 tablespoon prepared horseradish
Juice of 1 lemon
Hot pepper sauce

Combine ketchup, chili-garlic paste, horseradish and lemon juice in small bowl. Add hot pepper sauce to taste. Cover and refrigerate 1 hour. *Makes about 1 cup sauce*

Baked Cod with Tomatoes and Olives

    1 pound cod fillets (about 4 fillets), cut into 2-inch pieces
      Salt and black pepper
    1 can (about 14 ounces) diced tomatoes
    2 tablespoons chopped pitted black olives
    1 teaspoon minced garlic
    2 tablespoons chopped fresh parsley

1. Preheat oven to 400°F. Spray 13×9-inch baking dish with nonstick cooking spray. Arrange cod fillets in dish; season with salt and pepper.

2. Combine tomatoes, olives and garlic in medium bowl. Spoon over fish.

3. Bake 20 minutes or until fish just begins to flake when tested with fork. Sprinkle with parsley.

Makes 4 servings

Mussels in Beer Broth

    2 tablespoons olive oil
    ⅓ cup chopped shallots
    4 cloves garlic, minced
    2 cups pale ale or other light-colored beer
    1 can (about 14 ounces) seasoned diced tomatoes
    ¼ cup chopped fresh parsley
    1 tablespoon chopped fresh thyme
    ½ teaspoon salt
    ¼ teaspoon red pepper flakes
    3 pounds mussels, scrubbed and debearded
      French bread (optional)

1. Heat oil in large saucepan or Dutch oven. Add shallots and garlic; cook and stir 3 minutes or until tender. Stir in beer, tomatoes, parsley, thyme, salt and red pepper flakes; bring to a boil over medium-high heat.

2. Add mussels to saucepan. Reduce heat to low; cover and simmer 5 to 7 minutes or until mussels open. Discard any unopened mussels. Serve with French bread, if desired.

Makes 4 servings

Corned Beef and Cabbage with Horseradish Mustard Sauce

1 large onion, cut into chunks

1½ cups baby carrots

16 small (1-inch) red potatoes* (about 1¼ pounds)

1 corned beef brisket (2 to 2½ pounds)

½ large head cabbage (1 pound), cut into 8 thin wedges

⅓ cup sour cream

⅓ cup mayonnaise

2 tablespoons Dijon mustard

2 tablespoons prepared horseradish

If 1-inch potatoes are not available, cut larger potatoes into halves or quarters as needed.

Slow Cooker Directions

1. Place onion, carrots and potatoes in slow cooker. Drain corned beef, reserving spice packet and juices from package. Place corned beef on vegetables; pour juices over beef and top with contents of spice packet. Add enough water to barely cover beef and vegetables (about 4 cups). Cover; cook on LOW 8 to 9 hours or on HIGH 5 to 6 hours or until corned beef is fork-tender.

2. Transfer corned beef to large sheet of heavy-duty foil; wrap tightly and set aside. Add cabbage to vegetables, pushing down into liquid. Increase heat to HIGH. Cover; cook on HIGH 30 to 40 minutes or until vegetables are tender.

3. Meanwhile, combine sour cream, mayonnaise, mustard and horseradish in small bowl; mix well. Reserve ½ cup of juices in slow cooker. Drain vegetables; transfer to serving platter. Thinly slice corned beef; arrange on platter and drizzle with reserved juices. Serve with horseradish mustard sauce. *Makes 6 to 8 servings*

Lamb and Potato Hot Pot

3 tablespoons canola oil, divided
1½ pounds boneless leg of lamb, cut into 1-inch cubes
4 medium onions, thinly sliced
3 carrots, thinly sliced
1 teaspoon chopped fresh thyme
2 tablespoons all-purpose flour
1¼ cups reduced-sodium chicken broth
¾ teaspoon salt, divided
¼ teaspoon black pepper
3 medium russet potatoes (12 ounces), peeled and thinly sliced
1 tablespoon butter, cut into small pieces

1. Preheat oven to 350°F. Spray 2-quart casserole with nonstick cooking spray.

2. Heat 2 tablespoons oil in large saucepan over medium-high heat. Add half of lamb; cook 4 to 5 minutes or until browned, turning occasionally. Transfer lamb to plate; repeat with remaining lamb.

3. Heat remaining 1 tablespoon oil in saucepan over medium-high heat. Add onions, carrots and thyme; cook 10 to 12 minutes or until onions are golden, stirring occasionally. Stir in lamb and any accumulated juices; cook 1 minute. Add flour; cook and stir 1 minute. Stir in broth, ½ teaspoon salt and pepper; bring to a boil and cook about 1 minute or until mixture starts to thicken. Transfer to prepared casserole.

4. Arrange potato slices in overlapping layer over lamb mixture, starting from sides of casserole and working in towards center. Sprinkle potatoes with remaining ¼ teaspoon salt; dot with butter. Cover tightly with foil.

5. Bake 1 hour. Uncover; bake 15 to 20 minutes or until potatoes just begin to brown at edges and lamb is tender.

Makes 4 to 6 servings

Stuffed Pork Tenderloin
with Apple Relish

6 tablespoons (¾ stick) butter
1 onion, chopped
3 cloves garlic
1 cup dry bread crumbs
1 tablespoon chopped fresh parsley
2 teaspoons minced fresh thyme
1 teaspoon minced fresh sage
½ teaspoon salt, divided
¼ teaspoon black pepper
1 egg, lightly beaten
3 to 4 tablespoons dry white wine or apple cider
2 pork tenderloins (about 1 pound each)
   Apple Relish (recipe follows)

1. Preheat oven to 450°F. Place rack in large roasting pan; spray with nonstick cooking spray.

2. Melt butter in large skillet. Add onion and garlic; cook and stir 2 to 3 minutes or until translucent. Add bread crumbs, parsley, thyme, sage, ¼ teaspoon salt and pepper; mix well. Stir in egg. Add enough wine to moisten stuffing.

3. Trim fat from tenderloins. Cut tenderloins in half horizontally about halfway through and open flat. Cover with plastic wrap; pound to ½-inch thickness.

4. Sprinkle tenderloins with remaining ¼ teaspoon salt. Spoon half of stuffing down center of each tenderloin. Close meat around stuffing; tie with cotton twine every 3 or 4 inches to secure. Place in prepared pan.

5. Bake 15 minutes. *Reduce oven temperature to 350°F;* bake 45 minutes or until cooked through (145°F). Meanwhile, prepare Apple Relish. Serve with pork.   *Makes 8 servings*

Apple Relish: Combine 3 large apples, cut into ½-inch pieces, ½ cup chopped green onions, ½ cup golden raisins, ¼ cup chopped crystallized ginger, ¼ cup cider vinegar, 3 tablespoons sugar and 1 tablespoon Irish whiskey in medium saucepan. Cook, partially covered, over medium heat 20 to 30 minutes or until apples are tender but not falling apart. Let cool. Stir in 1 tablepoon chopped fresh mint. Serve warm or cold.

Stuffed Pork Tenderloin with Apple Relish

Steak and Mushroom Pie

3 tablespoons butter
1½ pounds beef chuck steak, cut into 1-inch cubes
2 medium onions, chopped
3 stalks celery, cut into ½-inch slices
1 package (8 ounces) sliced white mushrooms
½ teaspoon dried thyme
½ cup red wine
¼ cup all-purpose flour
1 cup reduced-sodium beef broth
2 tablespoons tomato paste
1 tablespoon Dijon mustard
½ teaspoon salt
¼ teaspoon black pepper
1 refrigerated pie crust (half of 15-ounce package)
1 egg, lightly beaten

1. Spray deep-dish pie plate or 1½-quart baking dish with nonstick cooking spray. Melt 2 tablespoons butter in large saucepan over medium-high heat. Add half of beef; cook 4 to 5 minutes or until browned, turning occasionally. Transfer to plate; repeat with remaining beef.

2. Melt remaining 1 tablespoon butter in same saucepan over medium-high heat. Add onions, celery, mushrooms and thyme; cook and stir 4 to 5 minutes or until vegetables start to soften. Add wine; cook and stir 3 to 4 minutes or until almost evaporated. Add flour; cook and stir 1 minute. Stir in broth, tomato paste and mustard; bring to a boil. Reduce heat to medium-low; cover and simmer 60 to 70 minutes or until beef is very tender, stirring occasionally. Remove from heat; stir in salt and pepper. Transfer mixture to prepared baking dish; let cool 20 minutes.

3. Preheat oven to 400°F. Roll out pie crust on lightly floured surface to fit top of baking dish. Place crust over filling; decoratively flute or crimp edges. Brush crust with egg; cut several small slits in top of crust with tip of knife.

4. Bake 23 to 25 minutes or until crust is golden. Cool 5 minutes before serving.

Makes 4 to 6 servings

Spiced Honey Glazed Ham

1 smoked bone-in spiral-cut ham (8 pounds)
½ cup clover honey or other mild honey
2 tablespoons spicy brown mustard
2 tablespoons apple cider vinegar
1 teaspoon finely grated orange peel
¼ teaspoon black pepper
⅛ teaspoon ground cloves

1. Position rack in lower third of oven. Preheat oven to 325°F.

2. Line large baking sheet with heavy-duty foil; place wire rack over foil. Arrange ham on rack and cover loosely with foil. Pour 2 cups water into pan. Bake 1½ hours.

3. Meanwhile, prepare glaze. Combine honey, mustard, vinegar, orange peel, pepper and cloves in small saucepan; bring to a boil over medium-high heat. Remove from heat; set aside to cool.

4. Remove ham from oven; discard foil. *Increase oven temperature to 400°F.* Brush ham with glaze; bake, uncovered, 40 minutes or until shiny golden brown crust has formed, brushing with glaze every 10 minutes.

5. Remove ham to cutting board. Let stand 10 minutes before slicing.

Makes 12 to 14 servings

Smoked Sausage and Cabbage

   1 pound smoked sausage, cut into 2-inch pieces
   1 tablespoon olive oil
   6 cups coarsely chopped cabbage
   1 onion, cut into ½-inch wedges
   2 cloves garlic, minced
   ¾ teaspoon sugar
   ¼ teaspoon caraway seeds
   ¼ teaspoon salt
   ¼ teaspoon black pepper

1. Cook and stir sausage in large nonstick skillet over medium-high heat 3 minutes or until browned. Transfer to plate.

2. Heat oil in same skillet. Add cabbage, onion, garlic, sugar, caraway seeds, salt and pepper; cook and stir 5 minutes or until onion begins to brown. Add sausage; cover and cook 5 minutes. Remove from heat; let stand 5 minutes. *Makes 4 servings*

Lamb Chops with Mustard Sauce

   4 lamb loin chops (about 6 ounces each)
   1 teaspoon dried thyme
   ½ teaspoon salt
   ¼ teaspoon black pepper
   2 tablespoons canola or vegetable oil
   ¼ cup finely chopped shallots or sweet onion
   ¼ cup beef or chicken broth
   2 tablespoons Worcestershire sauce
 1½ tablespoons Dijon mustard

1. Sprinkle lamb with thyme, salt and pepper. Heat oil in large skillet over medium heat. Add lamb chops; cook 4 minutes per side. Transfer to plate.

2. Add shallots to skillet; cook 3 minutes, stirring occasionally. Add broth, Worcestershire sauce and mustard; cook over medium-low heat 5 minutes or until sauce thickens slightly, stirring occasionally.

3. Return lamb chops to skillet; cook 2 minutes for medium-rare or to desired doneness, turning once. *Makes 4 servings*

Smoked Sausage and Cabbage

Bacon, Onion and Stout Braised Short Ribs

4 pounds bone-in beef short ribs, well trimmed
  Salt and black pepper
1 tablespoon vegetable oil
6 ounces thick-cut bacon, chopped
1 large onion, halved and sliced
2 tablespoons all-purpose flour
2 tablespoons spicy brown mustard
1 tablespoon tomato paste
1 teaspoon salt
½ teaspoon ground black pepper
1 bottle (12 ounces) Irish stout
1 cup beef broth
1 bay leaf
2 tablespoons finely chopped parsley
  Hot mashed potatoes (optional)

Slow Cooker Directions

1. Season ribs with salt and pepper. Heat oil in large skillet over medium-high heat until almost smoking. Cook ribs in batches, turning to brown all sides. Transfer to slow cooker. Wipe out skillet with paper towel.

2. Cook bacon in same skillet over medium heat about 4 minutes or until crisp, stirring occasionally. Drain on paper towel-lined plate. Drain all but 1 tablespoon drippings from skillet.

3. Add onion to skillet; cook and stir until translucent. Add flour, mustard, tomato paste, 1 teaspoon salt and ½ teaspoon pepper; cook and stir 1 minute. Remove from heat; pour in stout, stirring to scrape up browned bits. Pour over short ribs. Add bacon, broth and bay leaf. Cover; cook on LOW 8 hours.

4. Skim fat from cooking liquid. Remove and discard bay leaf. Stir in parsley. Serve with mashed potatoes. *Makes 4 to 6 servings*

Tip: This recipe only gets better if made ahead and refrigerated overnight. It is also easier to skim any fat from the surface.

Beef Pot Roast

1 beef eye of round roast (about 2½ pounds), trimmed
1 can (about 14 ounces) reduced-sodium beef broth
2 cloves garlic
¼ teaspoon dried rosemary
¼ teaspoon dried thyme
¼ teaspoon dried sage
¼ teaspoon dried savory
4 small turnips, peeled and cut into wedges
10 ounces brussels sprouts (about 10 medium), trimmed
8 ounces baby carrots (about 2 cups)
4 ounces pearl onions (about 1 cup)
1 tablespoon water
2 teaspoons cornstarch

1. Heat Dutch oven over medium-high heat. Add roast; brown on all sides.

2. Add broth to Dutch oven; bring to a boil over high heat. Add garlic, rosemary, thyme, sage and savory. Reduce heat to low; cover and simmer 1½ hours.

3. Add turnips, brussels sprouts, carrots and onions; cover and cook over medium heat 25 to 30 minutes or until vegetables are tender. Remove meat and vegetables; arrange on serving platter. Cover with foil to keep warm.

4. Strain broth; return to Dutch oven. Stir water into cornstarch in small bowl until smooth. Stir cornstarch mixture into broth; bring to a boil over medium-high heat. Cook and stir 1 minute or until thick and bubbly. Serve gravy with pot roast and vegetables.

Makes 8 servings

Roasted Dijon Lamb with Herbs and Country Vegetables

20 cloves garlic, peeled (about 2 medium heads)
¼ cup Dijon mustard
2 tablespoons water
2 tablespoons fresh rosemary leaves
1 tablespoon fresh thyme
1¼ teaspoons salt, divided
1 teaspoon black pepper
4½ pounds boneless leg of lamb,* trimmed
1 pound parsnips, cut diagonally into ½-inch pieces
1 pound carrots, cut diagonally into ½-inch pieces
2 large onions, cut into ½-inch wedges
3 tablespoons extra virgin olive oil, divided

If unavailable, substitute packaged marinated lamb and rinse it off.

1. Combine garlic, mustard, water, rosemary, thyme, ¾ teaspoon salt and pepper in food processor; process until smooth. Place lamb in large bowl or baking pan. Spoon garlic mixture over lamb; cover and refrigerate at least 8 hours.

2. Preheat oven to 500°F. Line broiler pan with foil; top with broiler rack. Spray rack with nonstick cooking spray. Combine parsnips, carrots, onions and 2 tablespoons oil in large bowl; toss to coat. Spread evenly on broiler rack; top with lamb.

3. Roast 15 minutes. *Reduce oven temperature to 325°F.* Roast 1 hour and 20 minutes or until internal temperature reaches 155°F for medium or to desired doneness.

4. Transfer lamb to cutting board; let stand 10 minutes. Continue roasting vegetables 10 minutes.

5. Transfer vegetables to large bowl. Add remaining 1 tablespoon oil and ½ teaspoon salt; toss to coat. Thinly slice lamb and serve with vegetables.   *Makes 8 to 10 servings*

Cider Pork and Onions

4 to 4½ pounds bone-in pork shoulder roast (pork butt)
2 to 3 tablespoons vegetable oil
4 to 5 medium onions, sliced (about 4 cups)
1 teaspoon salt, divided
4 cloves garlic, minced
3 sprigs fresh rosemary
½ teaspoon black pepper
2 to 3 cups apple cider

1. Preheat oven to 325°F. Heat 2 tablespoons oil in Dutch oven over medium-high heat. Add pork; brown on all sides. Remove to plate.

2. Add onions and ½ teaspoon salt to Dutch oven; cook and stir 5 minutes or until translucent, adding additional oil as needed to prevent scorching. Add garlic; cook and stir 1 minute. Add pork and rosemary; sprinkle with remaining ½ teaspoon salt and pepper. Add cider to come about halfway up sides of pork.

3. Cover and bake 2 to 2½ hours or until very tender. (Meat should be almost falling off bones.) Remove to serving platter; keep warm.

4. Remove rosemary sprigs from Dutch oven. Boil liquid in Dutch oven over medium-high heat about 20 minutes or until reduced by half; skim fat. Season with additional salt and pepper, if desired. Cut pork; serve with sauce. *Makes 8 servings*

Sirloin with Mushrooms and Whiskey-Cream Sauce

2 tablespoons butter
1 tablespoon vegetable oil
8 ounces cremini mushrooms, sliced
1½ pounds sirloin steak
½ teaspoon salt
¼ teaspoon black pepper
½ cup Irish whiskey
½ cup whipping cream
½ cup reduced-sodium beef broth
Chopped fresh chives

1. Heat butter and oil in large skillet over medium-high heat. Add mushrooms; cook and stir 8 minutes or until liquid evaporates. Remove to small bowl.

2. Sprinkle both sides of steak with salt and pepper. Add to skillet; cook about 3 minutes per side or to desired doneness. Remove to serving plate; keep warm.

3. Add whiskey to skillet; cook and stir 2 minutes, scraping up browned bits from bottom of skillet. Add cream and broth; cook and stir 3 minutes. Stir in any accumulated juices from steak.

4. Return mushrooms to skillet; cook and stir 2 minutes or until sauce thickens. Pour sauce over steak; garnish with chives. *Makes 4 servings*

Sirloin with Mushrooms and Whiskey-Cream Sauce

Rack of Lamb

½ cup Irish stout
2 tablespoons Dijon mustard
2 tablespoons chopped fresh parsley
2 tablespoons chopped fresh thyme
1 French-cut rack of lamb (8 ribs, 1½ pounds)
½ teaspoon coarse salt
½ teaspoon black pepper

1. Position rack in center of oven. Preheat oven to 400°F. Spray broiler pan and rack with nonstick cooking spray.

2. Combine stout, mustard, parsley and thyme in small bowl.

3. Sprinkle both sides of lamb with salt and pepper; spread with stout mixture. Place lamb, bone side down, on prepared broiler rack.

4. Bake 45 minutes or until internal temperature reaches 145°F for medium-rare or to desired doneness. Cover with foil; let stand 10 minutes before slicing. Cut into 8 pieces.

Makes 4 servings

TIP To help prevent too much browning on the tips of the bones, cover them with foil. (Cover the tips only, not the entire rack.)

Beef Stew

2 tablespoons olive or vegetable oil

3 pounds beef chuck, trimmed and cut into 2-inch chunks

2 teaspoons salt

½ teaspoon black pepper

3 medium sweet or yellow onions, halved and sliced

6 medium carrots, cut into ½-inch pieces

8 ounces sliced white mushrooms

¼ pound smoked ham, cut into ¼-inch pieces

2 tablespoons minced garlic

1 can (about 15 ounces) Irish stout

1 can (about 14 ounces) reduced-sodium beef broth

1 teaspoon sugar

1 teaspoon dried thyme

1 teaspoon Worcestershire sauce

⅓ cup cold water

2 tablespoons cornstarch

3 tablespoons chopped fresh parsley

Hot cooked noodles or steamed red potatoes (optional)

1. Heat oil in Dutch oven over medium-high heat. Add half of beef; sprinkle with salt and pepper. Cook about 8 minutes or until browned on all sides. Remove to bowl; repeat with remaining beef.

2. Add onions; cook and stir over medium heat about 10 minutes. Stir in carrots, mushrooms, ham and garlic; cook and stir 10 minutes or until vegetables are softened, scraping up browned bits from bottom of Dutch oven.

3. Return beef to Dutch oven; add stout and broth. (Liquid should just cover beef and vegetables; add water if needed.) Stir in sugar, thyme and Worcestershire sauce; bring to a boil. Reduce heat to low; cover and simmer 2 hours or until beef is fork-tender.

4. Skim fat. Stir water into cornstarch in small bowl until smooth. Stir into stew; simmer 5 minutes. Stir in parsley. Serve with noodles, if desired. *Makes 8 servings*

Sage-Roasted Pork with Rutabaga

1 bunch fresh sage
4 cloves garlic, minced (2 tablespoons)
1½ teaspoons coarse salt, divided
1 teaspoon coarsely ground pepper, divided
5 tablespoons extra virgin olive oil, divided
1 boneless pork loin roast (2 to 2½ pounds)
2 medium or 1 large rutabaga (1 to 1½ pounds)
4 carrots, cut into 1½-inch pieces

1. Chop enough sage to measure 2 tablespoons; reserve remaining sage. Mash chopped sage, garlic, ½ teaspoon salt and ½ teaspoon pepper in small bowl to form paste. Stir in 2 tablepoons oil.

2. Score fatty side of pork roast with sharp knife, making cuts about ¼ inch deep. Rub herb paste into cuts and onto all sides of pork. Place pork on large plate; cover and refrigerate 1 to 2 hours.

3. Preheat oven to 400°F. Spray large roasting pan with nonstick cooking spray. Cut rutabaga into halves or quarters; peel and cut into 1½-inch pieces. Place rutabaga and carrots in large bowl. Drizzle with remaining 3 tablespoons oil and sprinkle with remaining 1 teaspoon salt and ½ teaspoon pepper; toss to coat.

4. Arrange vegetables in single layer in prepared pan. Place pork on top of vegetables, scraping any remaining herb paste from plate into roasting pan. Tuck 3 sprigs of remaining sage into vegetables.

5. Bake 15 minutes. *Reduce oven temperature to 325°F.* Bake 45 minutes to 1 hour 15 minutes or until internal temperature reaches 145°F and pork is barely pink in center, stirring vegetables once during cooking time. Let pork rest 5 minutes before slicing.

Makes 4 to 6 servings

Tip: Rutabagas can be difficult to cut—they are a tough vegetable and are slippery on the outside because they are waxed. Cutting them into large pieces (halves or quarters) before peeling and chopping makes them easier to manage.

Irish Stout Chicken

2 tablespoons vegetable oil
1 medium onion, chopped
2 cloves garlic, minced
1 whole chicken (3 to 4 pounds), cut into serving pieces
5 carrots, chopped
2 parsnips, peeled and chopped
1 teaspoon dried thyme
¾ teaspoon salt
½ teaspoon black pepper
¾ cup Irish stout
8 ounces sliced white mushrooms
¾ cup frozen peas

1. Heat oil in large skillet over medium heat. Add onion and garlic; cook and stir 3 minutes or until tender. Remove to small bowl.

2. Cook chicken in single layer in same skillet over medium-high heat 5 minutes per side or until lightly browned.

3. Add onion mixture, carrots, parsnips, thyme, salt and pepper to skillet. Pour in stout; bring to a boil over high heat. Reduce heat to low; cover and simmer 35 minutes.

4. Stir in mushrooms and peas; cover and cook 10 minutes. Uncover skillet; cook over medium heat 10 minutes or until sauce is slightly thickened and chicken is cooked through (165°F). *Makes 4 servings*

Roast Duck with Apple Stuffing

1 duck (about 5 pounds)
Coarse salt and black pepper
2 tablespoons butter
1 small onion, chopped
2 stalks celery, chopped
3 apples, peeled and cut into bite-size pieces
½ cup chopped mixed dried fruit (prunes, apricots, etc.)
5 to 6 fresh sage leaves (tear large leaves in half)
1 cup dried bread cubes (¼- to ½-inch pieces)
Juice of 1 lemon
1 cup plus 1 tablespoon chicken broth, divided
⅔ cup dry white wine

1. Discard neck, giblets and liver from duck (or reserve for another use); trim excess fat. Rinse duck thoroughly; dry with paper towels. Generously season outside of duck and cavity with salt and pepper. Place duck on rack in roasting pan. Refrigerate, uncovered, 1 to 3 hours until ready to cook.

2. For stuffing, melt butter in medium skillet over medium-high heat. Add onion and celery; cook and stir 2 minutes. Add apples, dried fruit and sage; cook and stir 10 minutes or until apples and vegetables are softened. Combine apple mixture and bread cubes in medium bowl; season with ½ teaspoon salt and ¼ teaspoon pepper. Stir in lemon juice. If stuffing seems dry, add 1 tablespoon broth.

3. Preheat oven to 350°F. Spoon stuffing into duck cavity, packing tightly. Tie legs together with kitchen twine. Cut through duck skin in crisscross pattern over breast and legs, being careful to only cut though skin and fat layer (about ¼ inch thick), but not into duck flesh. (Cuts will help render duck fat and make skin crisp.)

4. Roast 1½ to 2 hours or until juices run clear and thermometer inserted into leg joint registers 175°F, rotating pan every 20 minutes. (Temperature of stuffing should reach 165°F.) Remove duck to cutting board. Pour off fat from pan; refrigerate or freeze for another use or discard.

5. Place roasting pan over medium-high heat. Add wine; cook and stir 5 minutes or until wine is reduced by half, scraping up browned bits from bottom of pan. Add remaining 1 cup broth; cook and stir 2 minutes. Strain sauce; serve with duck and stuffing.

Makes 4 servings

Tip: Ducks are large birds but have very little meat for their size. One duck can serve four with side dishes. For a bigger group, double the stuffing recipe and roast two ducks.

Herb Roasted Chicken

1 whole chicken (3 to 4 pounds)
1¼ teaspoons salt, divided
½ teaspoon black pepper, divided
1 lemon, cut into quarters
4 sprigs fresh rosemary, divided
4 sprigs fresh thyme, divided
4 cloves garlic, peeled
2 tablespoons olive oil

1. Preheat oven to 425°F. Place chicken, breast side up, in shallow roasting pan. Season cavity of chicken with ½ teaspoon salt and ¼ teaspoon pepper. Fill cavity with lemon quarters, 2 sprigs rosemary, 2 sprigs thyme and garlic cloves.

2. Chop remaining rosemary and thyme leaves; combine with oil, remaining ¾ teaspoon salt and ¼ teaspoon pepper in small bowl. Brush mixture over chicken.

3 . Roast 30 minutes. *Reduce oven temperature to 375°F;* roast 35 to 45 minutes more or until cooked through (165°F). Let stand 10 to 15 minutes before carving.

Makes 4 to 5 servings

Crispy Mustard Chicken

4 bone-in chicken breasts
Salt and black pepper
⅓ cup Dijon mustard
½ cup panko bread crumbs or coarse dry bread crumbs

1. Preheat oven to 350°F. Spray rack of broiler pan or shallow baking pan with nonstick cooking spray.

2. Remove skin from chicken. Season chicken with salt and pepper; place on prepared rack. Bake 20 minutes.

3. Brush chicken generously with mustard. Sprinkle with panko and gently press into mustard. Bake 20 to 25 minutes or until chicken is cooked through (165°F).

Makes 4 servings

Chicken Scallopini with Swiss Chard

2 slices bacon, chopped
1 cup chopped sweet or yellow onion
1 pound Swiss chard, trimmed and coarsely chopped (6 cups packed)
1 egg white
1 teaspoon water
¼ cup unseasoned bread crumbs
1 tablespoon olive oil
1 pound chicken cutlets*
Lemon wedges (optional)

Chicken cutlets are fresh boneless skinless chicken breast halves that have been sliced about ⅓ inch thick. If they aren't available, pound four (4-ounce) chicken breast halves to ⅓-inch thickness.

1. Cook bacon and onion in large saucepan over medium heat 6 to 8 minutes or until onion is golden brown. Add chard; cover and simmer 2 minutes to wilt. Stir mixture; cook, uncovered, 10 minutes or until chard is tender, stirring occasionally.

2. Meanwhile, beat egg white and water in shallow dish. Place bread crumbs in separate shallow dish. Dip each chicken cutlet first in egg white, letting excess drip off, then in bread crumbs, coating both sides lightly and using all crumbs.

3. Heat oil in large nonstick skillet over medium-high heat. Add chicken cutlets; cook 3 minutes or until golden brown on bottom. Turn chicken; cook over medium heat 3 to 4 minutes or until golden brown and no longer pink in center. (Watch carefully to avoid burning.) Serve chicken over chard mixture; garnish with lemon wedges.

Makes 4 servings

Chicken and Herb Stew

½ cup all-purpose flour
½ teaspoon salt
¼ teaspoon black pepper
¼ teaspoon paprika
4 chicken drumsticks
4 chicken thighs
2 tablespoons olive oil
12 ounces new potatoes, quartered
2 carrots, quartered lengthwise and cut into 3-inch pieces
1 green bell pepper, cut into thin strips
¾ cup chopped onion
2 cloves garlic, minced
1¾ cups water
¼ cup dry white wine
2 chicken bouillon cubes
1 tablespoon chopped fresh oregano
1 teaspoon chopped fresh rosemary
2 tablespoons chopped fresh Italian parsley (optional)

1. Combine flour, salt, black pepper and paprika in shallow dish. Coat chicken with flour mixture, shaking off excess.

2. Heat oil in large skillet over medium-high heat. Add chicken; cook 10 minutes or until browned on both sides, turning once. Transfer to plate.

3. Add potatoes, carrots, bell pepper, onion and garlic to skillet; cook and stir 5 minutes or until lightly browned. Add water, wine and bouillon; cook 1 minute, stirring to scrape up browned bits from bottom of skillet. Stir in oregano and rosemary.

4. Place chicken on top of vegetable mixture, turning several times to coat. Cover and simmer 45 to 50 minutes or until chicken is cooked through (165°F), turning occasionally. Garnish with parsley.

Makes 4 servings

Pan-Roasted Chicken Breasts

4 boneless skin-on chicken breasts (about 6 ounces each)
   Salt and black pepper
2 tablespoons vegetable oil
1 medium shallot, finely chopped (about ¼ cup)
1 tablespoon all-purpose flour
½ cup India Pale Ale
½ cup reduced-sodium chicken broth
¼ cup whipping cream
1 teaspoon Dijon mustard
½ teaspoon finely chopped fresh thyme
¼ teaspoon salt
⅛ teaspoon black pepper
½ cup (2 ounces) shredded Gruyère or Emmental cheese

1. Preheat oven to 375°F.

2. Season both sides of chicken breasts with salt and pepper. Heat oil in large ovenproof skillet over medium-high heat until almost smoking. Add chicken, skin side down; cook 8 to 10 minutes or until skin is golden brown. Turn chicken; transfer skillet to oven. Roast about 15 minutes or until no longer pink in center. Remove chicken to plate; tent with foil to keep warm.

3. Add shallot to skillet; cook and stir over medium heat until softened. Add flour; cook and stir 1 minute. Add ale; cook until reduced by half, stirring to scrape up browned bits from bottom of skillet. Stir in broth, cream, mustard, thyme, ¼ teaspoon salt and ⅛ teaspoon pepper; cook until slightly thickened.

4. Remove from heat; whisk in cheese until melted and smooth. Spoon sauce over chicken. Serve immediately.

Makes 4 servings

Roasted Chicken Thighs with Mustard-Cream Sauce

8 bone-in skin-on chicken thighs
¾ teaspoon black pepper, divided
¼ teaspoon plus ⅛ teaspoon salt, divided
2 teaspoons vegetable oil
2 shallots, thinly sliced
½ Granny Smith apple, peeled and cut into ¼-inch pieces
½ cup chicken broth
½ cup whipping cream
1 tablespoon spicy brown mustard
½ teaspoon chopped fresh thyme

1. Preheat oven to 400°F.

2. Sprinkle both sides of chicken with ½ teaspoon pepper and ¼ teaspoon salt. Heat oil in large ovenproof skillet over medium-high heat. Add chicken, skin side down; cook 8 to 10 minutes or until skin is golden brown. Remove chicken to plate; drain excess fat from skillet.

3. Return chicken to skillet, skin side up. Transfer to oven; roast about 25 minutes or until chicken is cooked through (165°F.) Remove to clean plate; tent with foil to keep warm.

4. Drain all but 1 tablespoon fat from skillet; heat over medium heat. Add shallots and apple; cook and stir about 8 minutes or until tender. Stir in broth; cook over medium-high heat about 1 minute or until reduced by half, scraping up browned bits from bottom of skillet. Add cream, mustard, thyme, remaining ¼ teaspoon pepper and ⅛ teaspoon salt; cook and stir about 2 minutes or until slightly thickened. Spoon sauce over chicken. Serve immediately.

Makes 4 servings

SIDE DISHES

Stovies with Bacon

3 medium russet potatoes (about 1½ pounds), peeled
6 slices bacon
2 large onions, halved vertically and sliced
4 teaspoons butter
½ teaspoon salt
⅛ teaspoon black pepper
⅓ cup water

1. Place potatoes in large saucepan; add cold water to cover by 2 inches. Bring to a boil over medium-high heat; cook 15 minutes or until partially cooked. Drain; let stand until cool enough to handle. Cut potatoes into ½-inch-thick slices.

2. Cook bacon in large skillet over medium-high heat 6 to 7 minutes or until crisp, turning occasionally. Drain on paper towel-lined plate. Chop bacon; set aside.

3. Drain all but 3 tablespoons drippings from skillet; heat over medium heat. Add onions; cook 8 to 9 minutes or until softened but not browned, stirring occasionally. Transfer onions to small bowl.

4. Add butter to skillet; heat over medium heat until melted. Add potatoes; sprinkle with salt and pepper. Top with onions and pour in water; cover and cook 5 minutes. Stir in bacon; cook, uncovered, 10 to 12 minutes or until potatoes are tender and browned, stirring occasionally.

Makes 4 servings

Classic Irish Salad

Dressing

> 3 tablespoons mayonnaise
> 1 tablespoon Dijon mustard
> 1 tablespoon canola oil
> 1 tablespoon cider vinegar
> 2 teaspoons sugar
> ¼ teaspoon salt
> ⅛ teaspoon black pepper

Salad

> 6 cups torn romaine lettuce
> 2 cups baby arugula
> 1 large cucumber, halved lengthwise and sliced
> 4 radishes, thinly sliced
> 3 tablespoons chopped chives
> 2 hard-cooked eggs, cut into wedges
> 2 bottled pickled beets, quartered

1. For dressing, whisk mayonnaise, mustard, oil, vinegar, sugar, salt and pepper in small bowl until well blended.

2. For salad, toss romaine, arugula, cucumber, radishes and chives in large bowl. Divide among four plates; top with egg wedges and beet quarters. Serve dressing separately or drizzle over salads just before serving. *Makes 4 servings*

Potato Cakes with Brussels Sprouts

2½ pounds Yukon Gold potatoes, peeled and cut into 1-inch cubes
6 tablespoons butter, melted
⅓ cup milk, warmed
2 teaspoons salt
½ teaspoon black pepper
3 tablespoons vegetable oil, divided
12 ounces brussels sprouts, ends trimmed, thinly sliced
4 green onions, thinly sliced diagonally

1. Place potatoes in large saucepan; add cold water to cover by 2 inches. Bring to a boil over high heat. Reduce heat to medium-low; cover and simmer about 10 minutes or until potatoes are tender. Drain.

2. Return potatoes to saucepan; mash with potato masher until slightly chunky. Stir in butter, milk, salt and pepper until well blended; set aside.

3. Heat 1 tablespoon oil in large nonstick skillet over medium-high heat. Add brussels sprouts; cook about 8 minutes or until tender and lightly browned, stirring occasionally. Stir brussels sprouts and green onions into potato mixture. Wipe out skillet with paper towel.

4. Heat 1 tablespoon oil in skillet over medium heat. Drop potato mixture into skillet by ½ cupfuls, spacing potato cakes about ½ inch apart. (Use spoon to remove mixture from cup if necessary.) Cook about 3 minutes per side or until cakes are browned and crisp, pressing down lightly with spatula. Transfer to platter; tent with foil to keep warm. Repeat with remaining 1 tablespoon oil and potato mixture.   *Makes 12 potato cakes*

Mashed Carrots and Parsnips

1 medium russet potato (8 ounces), peeled and cut into 1-inch pieces
3 parsnips (12 ounces), peeled and cut into 1-inch pieces
3 carrots (12 ounces), cut into 1-inch pieces
1 tablespoon honey
¼ cup (½ stick) butter, softened
½ teaspoon salt
¼ teaspoon black pepper

1. Place potato in large saucepan; add cold water to cover by 3 inches. Bring to a boil over medium-high heat; cook about 7 minutes or until potato is partially cooked.

2. Add parsnips, carrots, and honey to saucepan; return to a boil. Cook 16 to 18 minutes or until vegetables are tender. Drain vegetables; return to saucepan. Add butter, salt and pepper; mash until smooth. Serve hot. *Makes 4 to 6 servings*

Rhubarb Chutney

1 cup coarsely chopped peeled apple
½ cup sugar
¼ cup water
¼ cup dark raisins
1 teaspoon grated lemon peel
2 cups sliced rhubarb (½-inch pieces)
3 tablespoons coarsely chopped pecans
2 to 3 teaspoons white vinegar
¾ teaspoon ground cinnamon (optional)

1. Combine apple, sugar, water, raisins and lemon peel in medium saucepan; cook over medium heat until sugar is dissolved, stirring constantly. Reduce heat to low; simmer, uncovered, about 5 minutes or until apple is almost tender.

2. Stir in rhubarb and pecans; bring to a boil over high heat. Reduce heat to low; simmer 8 to 10 minutes or until mixture is reduced to 1 cup, stirring occasionally. Stir in vinegar and cinnamon, if desired, during last 2 minutes of cooking.

3. Remove from heat; cool to room temperature. Cover and refrigerate until ready to serve. *Makes about 1 cup chutney*

Mashed Carrots and Parsnips

Tangy Red Cabbage with Apple and Bacon

8 slices Irish or thick-cut bacon
1 large onion, sliced
½ small head red cabbage (1 pound), thinly sliced
1 tablespoon sugar
1 Granny Smith apple, peeled and sliced
2 tablespoons cider vinegar
½ teaspoon salt
¼ teaspoon black pepper

1. Heat large skillet over medium-high heat. Add bacon; cook 6 to 8 minutes or until crisp, turning occasionally. Drain on paper towel-lined plate. Coarsely chop bacon.

2. Drain all but 2 tablespoons drippings from skillet. Add onion; cook and stir over medium-high heat 2 to 3 minutes or until onion begins to soften. Add cabbage and sugar; cook and stir 4 to 5 minutes or until cabbage wilts. Stir in apple; cook 3 minutes or until crisp-tender. Stir in vinegar; cook 1 minute or until absorbed.

3. Stir in bacon, salt and pepper; cook 1 minute or until heated through. Serve warm or at room temperature. *Makes 4 servings*

Onions Baked in Their Papers

4 medium yellow onions with skins intact (about 2½ inches in diameter)
1½ teaspoons mixed dried herbs such as thyme, sage and tarragon leaves
1 teaspoon sugar
½ teaspoon salt
Dash red pepper flakes
¼ cup (½ stick) butter, melted
½ cup fresh bread crumbs

1. Preheat oven to 400°F. Line 8- or 9-inch square baking pan with foil. Cut off stem and root ends of onions. Cut 1½-inch cone-shaped indentation in top of each onion with paring knife. Arrange onions on root ends in prepared pan.

2. Stir herbs, sugar, salt and red pepper flakes into melted butter in small bowl. Add bread crumbs; mix well. Spoon crumb mixture evenly into indentations in onions.

3. Bake about 1 hour or until fork-tender. Serve immediately. *Makes 4 servings*

Tangy Red Cabbage with Apple and Bacon

Boxty Pancakes

2 medium russet potatoes (1 pound), peeled, divided
⅔ cup all-purpose flour
1 teaspoon baking powder
½ teaspoon salt
⅔ cup low-fat buttermilk
3 tablespoons butter

1. Cut 1 potato into 1-inch chunks; place in small saucepan and add cold water to cover by 2 inches. Bring to a boil over medium-high heat; cook 14 to 18 minutes or until tender. Drain potato; return to saucepan and mash. Transfer to medium bowl.

2. Shred remaining potato on large holes of box grater; add to bowl with mashed potato. Stir in flour, baking powder and salt until blended. Stir in buttermilk.

3. Melt 1 tablespoon butter in large nonstick skillet over medium heat. Drop 4 slightly heaping tablespoonfuls of batter into skillet; flatten into 2½-inch circles. Cook about 4 minutes per side or until golden and puffed. Remove to plate; cover to keep warm. Repeat with remaining butter and batter. Serve immediately.

Makes 4 servings (16 to 20 pancakes)

Serving Suggestion: Serve with melted butter, sour cream or maple syrup.

Kale with Lemon and Garlic

1 tablespoon olive or vegetable oil
3 cloves garlic, minced
2 bunches kale or Swiss chard (1 to 1¼ pounds), tough stems removed and discarded, leaves thinly sliced
½ cup reduced-sodium chicken or vegetable broth
½ teaspoon salt
¼ teaspoon black pepper
1 lemon, cut into 8 wedges

1. Heat oil in large saucepan over medium heat. Add garlic; cook and stir 3 minutes. Add kale and broth; cover and simmer 7 minutes. Stir kale; reduce heat to medium-low. Cover and simmer 8 to 10 minutes or until kale is tender.

2. Stir in salt and pepper. Squeeze lemon wedge over each serving. *Makes 8 servings*

Braised Leeks

3 to 4 large leeks (1½ to 2 pounds)
¼ cup (½ stick) butter
¼ teaspoon salt
¼ teaspoon pepper
¼ cup dry white wine
¼ cup reduced-sodium chicken or vegetable broth
3 to 4 sprigs parsley

1. Trim green stem ends of leeks; remove any damaged outer leaves. Cut leeks lengthwise up to, but not through, root ends to hold leeks together. Rinse leeks in cold water, separating layers to remove embedded dirt. Cut leeks crosswise into 3-inch lengths; cut off and discard root ends.

2. Melt butter in skillet large enough to hold leeks in single layer over medium-high heat. Arrange leeks in skillet in crowded layer, keeping pieces together as much as possible. Cook about 8 minutes or until leeks begin to color and soften, turning with tongs once or twice. Sprinkle with salt and pepper.

3. Add wine, broth and parsley; bring to a simmer. Cover and cook over low heat 20 minutes or until leeks are very tender. Remove parsley sprigs before serving.

Makes 4 servings

Serving Suggestion: Top the braised leeks with toasted bread crumbs, cheese or crisp crumbled bacon for an extra-rich side dish.

TIP Leeks often contain a lot of embedded dirt between their layers, so they need to be washed thoroughly. It's easiest to slice up to—but not through—the root ends before slicing or chopping so the leeks hold together while washing them.

Colcannon with Spinach and Parsnips

3 medium russet potatoes (1½ pounds), peeled and cut into 1-inch pieces
3 parsnips (12 ounces), peeled and cut into 1-inch pieces
⅔ cup milk
5 tablespoons butter, plus additional for serving
¾ teaspoon salt
¼ teaspoon ground black pepper
3 cups baby spinach

1. Combine potatoes and parsnips in large saucepan; add cold water to cover by 2 inches. Bring to a boil over medium-high heat; cook 18 to 20 minutes or until tender. Drain vegetables; return to saucepan.

2. Heat milk in small saucepan over medium-high heat until hot. Add butter, salt and pepper; cook until butter is melted.

3. Pour three fourths of milk mixture into saucepan with vegetables; mash until smooth. Stir in spinach until well combined. Add remaining milk mixture as needed to reach desired consistency. Transfer to serving dish; top with additional melted butter, if desired.

Makes 4 to 6 servings

Yorkshire Pudding

1 cup milk
2 eggs
½ teaspoon salt
1 cup all-purpose flour
¼ cup reserved drippings from roast or melted butter

1. Combine milk, eggs and salt in blender or food processor; blend 15 seconds. Add flour; blend 2 minutes. Let batter stand in blender at room temperature 30 minutes to 1 hour.

2. Preheat oven to 450°F. Place meat drippings in 9-inch square baking pan. Heat in oven 5 minutes.

3. Blend batter 10 seconds; pour into hot drippings. *Do not stir.* Immediately return pan to oven. Bake 20 minutes. *Reduce oven temperature to 350°F;* bake 10 minutes or until pudding is golden brown and puffed. Cut into squares. Serve warm.

Makes 6 to 8 servings

Colcannon with Spinach and Parsnips

Beet and Arugula Salad

3 medium beets, trimmed
6 cups baby arugula
2 tablespoons finely chopped shallots
1 tablespoon white wine vinegar
1 teaspoon Dijon mustard
¼ teaspoon salt
⅛ teaspoon black pepper
3 tablespoons extra virgin olive oil
4 wedges (1 ounce each) aged Irish Cheddar cheese

1. Place beets in medium saucepan; add cold water to cover by 2 inches. Bring to a boil over medium-high heat; cook 35 to 40 minutes or until beets can be easily pierced with tip of knife. Drain beets; cool 15 minutes.

2. Peel beets; cut into ½-inch cubes. Transfer to medium bowl. Place arugula in separate medium bowl. Combine shallots, vinegar, mustard, salt and pepper in small bowl. Slowly whisk in oil until well blended. Toss beets with 1 tablespoon dressing. Toss arugula with remaining dressing.

3. Divide arugula among four plates. Top with beets; garnish with wedge of cheese. Serve immediately. *Makes 4 servings*

Green Cabbage Salad

2 tablespoons extra virgin olive oil
1 tablespoon cider vinegar
1 clove garlic, minced
½ teaspoon granulated sugar
¼ teaspoon salt
⅛ teaspoon black pepper
2 cups thinly sliced green cabbage

1. Combine all ingredients except cabbage in small jar with tight-fitting lid. Cover and shake until well blended.

2. Place cabbage in medium bowl. Add dressing; toss gently to coat. Let stand at least 10 minutes before serving. For milder flavor, refrigerate 1 hour. *Makes 2 servings*

Beet and Arugula Salad

Leek and Chive Champ

3 medium russet potatoes (1½ pounds), peeled and cut into 1-inch pieces
6 tablespoons butter, divided
2 large leeks, white and light green parts only, halved and sliced
½ cup milk
¼ cup chopped fresh chives
½ teaspoon salt
¼ teaspoon black pepper
½ cup French fried onions (optional)

1. Place potatoes in large saucepan; add cold water to cover by 2 inches. Bring to a boil over medium-high heat; cook 16 to 18 minutes or until tender. Drain and return to saucepan.

2. Meanwhile, melt 2 tablespoons butter in small skillet over medium heat. Add leeks; cook 5 to 6 minutes or until tender, stirring occasionally.

3. Heat milk in small saucepan over medium-high heat until hot. Add 2 tablespoons butter; cook until melted. Pour milk mixture into saucepan with potatoes; mash until smooth. Stir in leeks, chives, salt, and pepper; mix well.

4. Transfer to serving bowl; make large indentation in top of potatoes. Melt remaining 2 tablespoons butter; pour into indentation. Sprinkle with fried onions, if desired.

Makes 4 to 6 servings

Roasted Parsnips, Carrots and Red Onion

2 carrots (8 ounces), cut into 2-inch-long pieces
2 parsnips (8 ounces), cut into 2-inch-long pieces
¾ cup vertically sliced red onion (¼-inch slices)
1 tablespoon extra virgin olive oil
1 tablespoon balsamic vinegar
¼ teaspoon salt
⅛ teaspoon black pepper

1. Preheat oven to 425°F. Line large baking sheet with foil. Combine carrots, parsnips, onion, oil, vinegar, salt and pepper in large bowl; toss to coat. Transfer to prepared baking sheet; spread vegetables in single layer.

2. Roast about 30 minutes or until tender, stirring occasionally.

Makes 4 servings

Roasted Cauliflower with Cheddar Beer Sauce

1 large head cauliflower (about 2½ pounds), trimmed and cut into ½-inch florets
2 tablespoons vegetable oil, divided
½ teaspoon salt, divided
½ teaspoon black pepper
2 medium shallots, finely chopped
2 teaspoons all-purpose flour
½ cup Irish ale
1 tablespoon spicy brown mustard
1 tablespoon Worcestershire sauce
1½ cups (6 ounces) shredded Cheddar cheese

1. Preheat oven to 450°F. Line large baking sheet with foil.

2. Combine cauliflower, 1 tablespoon oil, ¼ teaspoon salt and pepper in medium bowl; toss to coat. Spread in single layer on prepared baking sheet. Roast about 25 minutes or until tender and lightly browned, stirring occasionally.

3. Meanwhile, prepare sauce. Heat remaining 1 tablespoon oil in medium saucepan over medium heat. Add shallots; cook and stir 3 to 4 minutes or until tender. Add flour and remaining ¼ teaspoon salt; cook and stir 1 minute. Add ale, mustard and Worcestershire sauce; bring to a simmer over medium-high heat. Reduce heat to medium-low; add cheese by ¼ cupfuls, stirring until cheese is melted before adding more. Cover and keep warm over low heat, stirring occasionally.

4. Transfer roasted cauliflower to serving bowl; top with cheese sauce. Serve immediately.

Makes 4 to 6 servings

Roasted Cauliflower with Cheddar Beer Sauce

Haggerty

8 slices bacon (about 8 ounces)
3 onions, thinly sliced
5 medium red potatoes (about 1¼ pounds), very thinly sliced
1½ cups (6 ounces) shredded Irish Cheddar cheese, divided
2 tablespoons butter, divided
Salt and black pepper

1. Preheat oven to 375°F.

2. Cook bacon in large ovenproof skillet over medium-high heat 6 to 7 minutes or until crisp, turning occasionally. Drain on paper towel-lined plate; crumble into medium bowl. Drain all but 1 tablespoon drippings from skillet.

3. Add onions to skillet; cook and stir over medium heat about 8 minutes or until translucent but not browned. Drain on paper towel-lined plate. Transfer to bowl with bacon; mix well.

3. Reserve ¼ cup cheese; set aside. Melt 1 tablespoon butter in same skillet or 8- to 9-inch casserole. Arrange one quarter of potato slices to cover bottom of skillet. Season with salt and pepper. Top with one third of bacon-onion mixture; sprinkle with one third of remaining cheese. Repeat layers twice. Top with remaining one quarter of potato slices; dot with remaining 1 tablespoon butter.

4. Cover with foil and bake 50 minutes. Uncover and bake 10 minutes or until potatoes are tender. *Turn oven to broil;* broil 2 to 3 minutes or until lightly browned. Sprinkle with reserved ¼ cup cheese Serve warm. *Makes 6 to 8 servings*

TIP Use a mandolin to slice the potatoes very thin (about ⅛ inch). Thicker pieces may require a longer cooking time.

Guinness Beef Stew

3 tablespoons vegetable oil
3 pounds boneless beef chuck roast, cut into 1-inch pieces
2 medium onions, chopped
2 stalks celery, chopped
3 tablespoons all-purpose flour
1 tablespoon minced garlic
1 tablespoon tomato paste
2 teaspoons chopped fresh thyme
1½ teaspoons salt
½ teaspoon black pepper
1 bottle (about 11 ounces) Guinness
1 cup reduced-sodium beef broth
3 carrots, peeled and cut into 1-inch chunks
4 small turnips (¾ pound), peeled and cut into 1-inch pieces
4 medium Yukon Gold potatoes (1 pound), peeled and cut into 1-inch pieces
¼ cup finely chopped fresh parsley

1. Preheat oven to 350°F. Heat 2 tablespoons oil in Dutch oven over medium-high heat until almost smoking. Add beef in two batches; cook about 10 minutes per batch or until browned on all sides. Remove beef to large plate.

2. Add remaining 1 tablespoon oil to Dutch oven; heat over medium heat. Add onions and celery; cook about 10 minutes or until onions are softened and translucent. Add flour, garlic, tomato paste, thyme, salt and pepper; cook and stir 1 minute. Add Guinness; use wooden spoon to scrape up browned bits from bottom of Dutch oven. Return beef to pan; stir in broth.

3. Cover and bake 1 hour. Stir in carrots, turnips and potatoes; cover and bake about 1 hour 20 minutes or until beef and vegetables are tender. Stir in parsley.

Makes 6 servings

Lamb and Mint Hand Pies

2 cups plus 1 tablespoon all-purpose flour, divided
1 teaspoon salt, divided
10 tablespoons cold butter, cut into small pieces
7 to 8 tablespoons ice water
1 pound ground lamb
1 small onion, finely chopped
1 carrot, finely chopped
½ cup reduced-sodium beef broth
1 teaspoon Dijon mustard
¼ teaspoon black pepper
1 tablespoon chopped fresh mint
½ cup (2 ounces) shredded Irish Cheddar cheese
1 egg, lightly beaten

1. For dough, combine 2 cups flour and ½ teaspoon salt in medium bowl. Cut in butter with pastry blender or two knives until mixture resembles coarse crumbs. Add water, 1 tablespoon at a time, stirring with fork until loose dough forms. Knead dough in bowl 1 to 2 times until it comes together. Divide dough into 4 pieces; press each into 4-inch disc. Wrap dough in plastic wrap; freeze 15 minutes.

2. Meanwhile, prepare filling. Heat large skillet over medium-high heat. Add lamb; cook 7 to 8 minutes or until lightly browned, stirring occasionally. Drain well; remove to plate. Add onion and carrot to skillet; cook 2 to 3 minutes or until vegetables start to soften, stirring occasionally. Stir in lamb; cook 1 minute. Add remaining 1 tablespoon flour; cook and stir 1 minute. Add broth, mustard, remaining ½ teaspoon salt and pepper; cook over medium heat about 2 minutes or until thickened. Remove from heat; stir in mint. Cool 10 minutes. Stir in cheese.

3. Position rack in center of oven. Preheat oven to 400°F. Line large baking sheet with parchment paper or spray with nonstick cooking spray.

4. Working with one disc at a time, roll out dough into 9-inch circle on lightly floured surface. Cut out 4 circles with 4-inch round cookie cutter (16 circles total). Place 8 dough circles on prepared baking sheet. Top each with ⅛ of lamb filling, leaving ½-inch border around edge of circle. Top with remaining dough circles, pressing edges to seal. Press edges again with tines of fork. Brush tops with egg; cut 1-inch slit in top of each pie with tip of knife.

5. Bake 28 to 30 minutes or until golden brown. Serve hot or at room temperature.

Makes 4 main-dish or 8 appetizer servings

Pub-Style Fish and Chips

¾ cup all-purpose flour, plus additional for dusting fish
½ cup flat beer
  Vegetable oil
3 large or 4 medium russet potatoes
1 egg, separated
1 pound cod fillets
  Salt
  Prepared tartar sauce
  Lemon wedges

1. Combine ¾ cup flour, beer and 2 teaspoons oil in small bowl. Cover and refrigerate 30 minutes or up to 2 hours.

2. Peel and cut potatoes into ¾-inch sticks. Place in large bowl of cold water. Pour at least 2 inches oil into deep heavy saucepan or deep fryer. Heat over medium heat to 320°F. Drain and thoroughly dry potatoes. Fry in batches 3 minutes or until slightly softened but not browned. Drain on paper towel-lined plate.

3. Stir egg yolk into reserved flour mixture. Beat egg white in medium bowl with electric mixer at medium-high speed until soft peaks form. Fold egg white into flour mixture. Season batter with pinch of salt.

4. Preheat oven to to 200°F. Heat oil to 365°F. Cut fish into pieces about 6 inches long and 2 to 3 inches wide. Remove any pin bones. Dust fish with flour; dip fish into batter, shaking off excess. Lower carefully into hot oil; cook 4 to 6 minutes or until batter is browned and fish is cooked through, turning once. Cook fish in batches; do not crowd pan. (Allow temperature of oil to return to 365°F between batches.) Drain on paper towel-lined plate; keep warm in oven.

5. Return potatoes to hot oil; cook in batches 5 minutes or until browned and crisp. Drain on paper towel-lined plate; sprinkle with salt. Serve fish with potatoes, tartar sauce and lemon wedges.

Makes 4 servings

Roasted Pork Chops with Apple and Cabbage

2 tablespoons olive oil, divided
½ medium onion, thinly sliced
2 cloves garlic, minced
1 teaspoon dried thyme
4 pork chops (6 to 8 ounces each), 1 inch thick
½ teaspoon salt
½ teaspoon black pepper, divided
¼ cup cider vinegar
1 tablespoon packed brown sugar
1 large McIntosh apple, peeled and chopped
½ (8-ounce) package shredded coleslaw mix

1. Preheat over to 375°F.

2. Heat 1 tablespoon oil in large ovenproof skillet over medium-high heat. Add onion; cook and stir 4 to 6 minutes or until tender Add garlic and thyme; cook and stir 30 seconds. Remove to small bowl.

3. Heat remaining 1 tablespoon oil in same skillet. Season pork chops with salt and ¼ teaspoon pepper. Add to skillet; cook 2 minutes per side or until browned. Remove pork chops to large plate.

4. Remove skillet from heat. Add vinegar, brown sugar and remaining ¼ teaspoon pepper; stir to dissolve sugar and scrape up browned bits from bottom of skillet. Add onion mixture, apple and coleslaw mix; do not stir.

5. Arrange pork chops on top of cabbage mixture, overlapping to fit. Cover and roast 15 minutes or until pork chops are barely pink in center.   *Makes 4 servings*

Ham with Dark Beer Gravy

1 fully cooked bone-in ham (about 6 pounds)
1 tablespoon Dijon mustard
2 cans (6 ounces each) pineapple juice
1 bottle (12 ounces) dark beer, such as porter
   Dark Beer Gravy (recipe follows)

1. Line large roasting pan with foil. Remove skin and excess fat from ham. Score ham in diamond pattern.

2. Place ham in prepared pan. Spread mustard over ham. Pour pineapple juice and beer over ham. Cover and refrigerate 8 hours.

3. Preheat oven to 350°F. Cook ham 1½ hours or until thermometer inserted into thickest part registers 140°F, basting every 30 minutes. Transfer to cutting board; cover and let stand 15 minutes before slicing.

4. Meanwhile, pour drippings from pan into 4-cup measuring cup. Let stand 5 minutes; skim and discard fat. Prepare Dark Beer Gravy; serve with ham.

Makes 10 to 12 servings

Dark Beer Gravy

¼ cup (½ stick) butter
¼ cup all-purpose flour
½ cup dark beer, such as porter
2 cups drippings from roasting pan
   Salt and black pepper

Melt butter in small saucepan over medium heat. Whisk in flour until blended. Cook 1 to 2 minutes, whisking constantly. Add beer to drippings; whisk into flour mixture. Cook until mixture is thickened and bubbly, whisking constantly. Season with salt and pepper.

Makes 2½ cups

Lamb Shanks Braised in Stout

4 lamb shanks, about 1 pound each
¼ cup vegetable oil, plus additional as needed
¼ cup all-purpose flour
1 large onion, chopped (about 2 cups)
4 cloves garlic, minced
  Salt and ground black pepper
3 sprigs *each* fresh rosemary and fresh thyme
1 bottle (about 11 ounces) Irish stout
2 to 3 cups reduced-sodium chicken broth
  Smashed Chat Potatoes (recipe follows)
1 tablespoon chopped fresh mint leaves

1. Preheat oven to 325°F. Trim excess fat from lamb. (Do not remove all fat or shanks will fall apart.) Dust lamb shanks with flour. Heat ¼ cup oil in large roasting pan over medium-high heat. Add lamb in batches; cook until browned on all sides. Remove to bowl.

2. Add oil to pan, if needed, to make about 2 tablespoons. Add onion; cook and stir 2 minutes. Add garlic; cook and stir 2 minutes. Return lamb shanks and any accumulated juices to pan. Sprinkle generously with salt and pepper. Tuck rosemary and thyme sprigs around lamb. Add stout to pan; pour in broth to almost cover lamb.

3. Cover and bake 2 hours or until lamb is very tender and almost falling off bones. Prepare Smashed Chat Potatoes. Remove lamb from pan; keep warm. Skim fat from juices in pan; boil until reduced by half. Strain sauce. Serve lamb over potatoes; sprinkle with mint.

Makes 4 servings

Smashed Chat Potatoes

1½ to 2 pounds unpeeled small white potatoes
1 tablespoon butter
  Salt and black pepper

Bring large saucepan of water to a boil Add potatoes; simmer over medium-low heat about 20 minutes or until fork-tender. Drain potatoes; return to saucepan and stir in butter until melted. Partially smash potatoes with fork or potato masher. Season with salt and pepper.

Note: In Irish dialect, "chat potatoes" are small white potatoes most often served whole and unpeeled after steaming or boiling. Any small potato may be substituted.

Sausage, Cabbage and Onions

2 tablespoons olive oil
1 pound pork sausage, cut in half lengthwise then cut diagonally into ¾-inch slices
1 onion, thinly sliced
2 teaspoons fennel seeds
1 teaspoon caraway seeds
1 clove garlic, minced
½ cup water
2 pounds red potatoes (about 5 medium), cut into ¾-inch pieces
1 pound cabbage (½ head), thinly sliced (6 cups)
1 bottle (12 ounces) lager beer or ale
½ teaspoon salt
¼ teaspoon black pepper

1. Heat oil in large skillet over medium heat. Add sausage; cook 5 minutes or until browned. Remove to plate with slotted spoon.

2. Add onion, fennel seeds, caraway seeds and garlic to skillet; cook and stir 2 to 3 minutes or until onion is translucent. Stir in ½ cup water, scraping up browned bits from bottom of skillet. Add potatoes and cabbage; cook 10 minutes or until cabbage is wilted, stirring occasionally.

3. Stir in beer; cover and cook over medium-low heat 15 minutes until potatoes are tender. Add salt and pepper; cook over medium heat 15 minutes until beer has reduced to sauce consistency. Return sausage to skillet; cook until heated through.　　*Makes 6 servings*

Beef Pot Pie

½ cup all-purpose flour
1 teaspoon salt, divided
½ teaspoon black pepper, divided
1½ pounds lean beef stew meat (1-inch pieces)
2 tablespoons olive oil
1 pound new red potatoes, cubed
2 cups baby carrots
1 cup frozen pearl onions, thawed
1 parsnip, peeled and cut into 1-inch pieces
1 cup stout
¾ cup beef broth
1 teaspoon chopped fresh thyme *or* ½ teaspoon dried thyme
1 refrigerated pie crust (half of 15-ounce package)

1. Preheat oven to 350°F. Combine flour, ½ teaspoon salt and ¼ teaspoon pepper in large resealable food storage bag. Add beef; shake to coat.

2. Heat oil in large skillet over medium-high heat. Add beef; brown on both sides, turning once. (Do not crowd meat in skillet; cook in batches if necessary.) Remove to 2½- to 3-quart casserole. Add potatoes, carrots, onions and parsnip; mix well.

3. Add stout, broth, thyme, remaining ½ teaspoon salt and ¼ teaspoon pepper to same skillet. Bring to a boil, scraping up browned bits from bottom of skillet. Pour into casserole.

4. Cover and bake 2½ to 3 hours or until meat is fork-tender, stirring once. Remove cover; let stand at room temperature 15 minutes.

5. *Increase oven temperature to 425°F.* Place pie crust over casserole and press edges to seal. Cut slits in crust to vent. Bake 15 to 20 minutes or until crust is golden brown. Cool slightly before serving. *Makes 4 to 6 servings*

Individual Beef Pot Pies: Instead of refrigerated pie crust, use 1 sheet puff pastry (half of 17-ounce package). Divide beef filling among six individual ovenproof serving dishes. Cut puff pastry to fit, press over moistened edges and crimp to seal. Brush tops with 1 lightly beaten egg yolk. Bake in preheated 400°F oven 15 to 20 minutes or until crust is puffed and golden.

Emerald Isle Lamb Chops

2 tablespoons vegetable or olive oil, divided
2 tablespoons coarse Dijon mustard
1 tablespoon Irish whiskey
1 tablespoon minced fresh rosemary
2 teaspoons minced garlic
1½ pounds loin lamb chops (about 6 chops)
½ teaspoon salt
½ teaspoon black pepper
¾ cup dry white wine
2 tablespoons black currant jam
1 to 2 tablespoons butter, cut into pieces

1. Combine 1 tablespoon oil, mustard, whiskey, rosemary and garlic in small bowl to form paste. Season lamb chops with salt and pepper; spread paste over both sides. Cover and marinate 30 minutes at room temperature or refrigerate 2 to 3 hours.

2. Heat remaining 1 tablespoon oil in large skillet over medium-high heat. Add lamb chops in single layer; cook 2 to 3 minutes per side or until desired doneness. Remove to serving plate and keep warm.

3. Drain excess fat from skillet. Add wine; cook and stir about 5 minutes, scraping up browned bits from bottom of skillet. Stir in jam until well blended. Remove from heat; stir in butter until melted. Serve sauce over lamb chops.   *Makes 4 to 6 servings*

Shepherd's Pie

    3 medium russet potatoes (1½ pounds), peeled and cut into 1-inch pieces
    5 tablespoons butter, divided
    ½ cup milk
    1 teaspoon salt, divided
    ½ teaspoon black pepper, divided
    2 medium onions, chopped
    2 medium carrots, finely chopped
    ½ teaspoon dried thyme
 1½ pounds ground lamb
    3 tablespoons tomato paste
    1 tablespoon Worcestershire sauce
 1½ cups reduced-sodium beef broth
    ½ cup frozen peas

1. Preheat oven to 350°F. Spray 1½-quart baking dish with nonstick cooking spray.

2. Place potatoes in large saucepan; add cold water to cover by 2 inches. Bring to a boil over medium-high heat; cook 16 to 18 minutes or until tender. Drain potatoes; return to saucepan.

3. Heat milk in small saucepan over medium-high heat until hot. Add 3 tablespoons butter, ½ teaspoon salt and ¼ teaspoon pepper; cook until butter is melted. Pour milk mixture into saucepan with potatoes; mash until smooth. Set aside.

3. Melt remaining 2 tablespoons butter in large nonstick skillet over medium heat. Add onions, carrots and thyme; cook 8 to 10 minutes until vegetables are softened but not browned, stirring occasionally. Add lamb; cook over medium-high heat 4 minutes or until no longer pink. Drain excess fat. Return skillet to heat; cook 5 to 6 minutes or until lamb is lightly browned. Add tomato paste and Worcestershire sauce; cook 1 minute. Stir in broth; bring to a boil and cook 7 to 8 minutes or until nearly evaporated. Stir in peas, remaining ½ teaspoon salt and ¼ teaspoon pepper; cook 30 seconds. Transfer mixture to prepared baking dish.

4. Spread mashed potatoes in even layer over lamb mixture; use spatula to swirl potatoes or fork to make crosshatch design on top.

5. Bake about 35 minutes or until filling is hot and bubbly and potatoes begin to brown.

Makes 4 to 6 servings

Mussels Steamed in Guinness

5 tablespoons butter, divided
½ cup chopped shallots
2 stalks celery, chopped
1 medium carrot, chopped
8 sprigs fresh parsley
⅔ cup Guinness
2 pounds mussels, scrubbed and debearded
   Crusty bread

1. Melt 1 tablespoon butter in large saucepan over medium-high heat. Add shallots, celery, carrot and parsley; cook 2 to 3 minutes or until vegetables begin to soften.

2. Add Guinness; bring to a boil and cook 2 minutes. Add mussels; cover and return to a boil. Cook 4 to 5 minutes or until mussels open. Uncover and cook 1 minute.

3. Remove from heat; discard any unopened mussels. Stir in remaining 4 tablespoons butter. Serve immediately in bowls with bread.   *Makes 4 appetizer or 2 main-dish servings*

Dublin Coddle

8 ounces brussels sprouts
4 potatoes (2 pounds), peeled and sliced ½ inch thick
1 pound Irish pork sausage,* cut into 1-inch slices
1 pound smoked ham, cut into cubes
3 onions, cut into 1-inch pieces
8 ounces baby carrots
1 teaspoon dried thyme
½ teaspoon black pepper

Irish pork sausage is similar to fresh garlic-flavored bratwurst. If unavailable, substitute 1 pound regular pork sausage and add 1 clove minced garlic with other ingredients in step 2.

1. Cut stem from each brussels sprout and pull off outer bruised leaves. Cut deep "X" into stem end of each sprout with paring knife.

2. Place potatoes, sausage, ham, brussels sprouts, onions, carrots, thyme and pepper in Dutch oven. Add water to cover; bring to a boil over high heat. Reduce heat to medium; cover and simmer 20 minutes. Uncover and cook 15 minutes or until vegetables are tender. Remove from heat. Cool slightly; skim fat from surface.   *Makes 8 to 10 servings*

Lamb and Vegetable Pie

2 tablespoons canola oil

1½ pounds boneless leg of lamb, cut into 1-inch cubes

3 medium russet potatoes (about 12 ounces), peeled and cut into 1-inch cubes

16 frozen pearl onions (about 1 cup)

1 cup frozen peas and carrots

3 tablespoons all-purpose flour

1½ cups reduced-sodium beef broth

3 tablespoons chopped fresh parsley

2 tablespoons tomato paste

2 teaspoons Worcestershire sauce

½ teaspoon salt

¼ teaspoon black pepper

1 refrigerated pie crust (half of 15-ounce package)

1 egg, lightly beaten

1. Spray 9-inch deep-dish pie plate or baking dish with nonstick cooking spray. Heat oil in large saucepan over medium-high heat. Add half of lamb; cook 4 to 5 minutes or until browned, turning occasionally. Remove lamb to plate; repeat with remaining lamb.

2. Add potatoes, onions and peas and carrots to saucepan; cook 2 minutes, stirring occasionally. Stir in lamb and any accumulated juices; cook 2 minutes. Add flour; cook and stir 1 minute. Stir in broth, parsley, tomato paste, Worcestershire sauce, salt and pepper; bring to a boil. Reduce heat to medium-low; cover and simmer about 30 minutes or until lamb and potatoes are tender, stirring occasionally. Transfer mixture to prepared pie plate; let cool 20 minutes.

3. Preheat oven to 400°F. Top lamb mixture with pie crust; flute edge. Brush crust with egg; cut several small slits in crust with tip of knife.

4. Bake 24 to 26 minutes or until crust is golden brown and filling is thick and bubbly. Cool 5 minutes before serving.

Makes 4 to 6 servings

BREAD

Irish Soda Bread

2½ cups all-purpose flour

1¼ cups whole wheat flour

1 cup currants

¼ cup sugar

4 teaspoons baking powder

2 teaspoons caraway seeds (optional)

1 teaspoon salt

½ teaspoon baking soda

½ cup (1 stick) butter, cut into small pieces

1⅓ to 1½ cups buttermilk

1. Preheat oven to 350°F. Grease large baking sheet or line with parchment paper.

2. Combine all-purpose flour, whole wheat flour, currants, sugar, baking powder, caraway seeds, if desired, salt and baking soda in large bowl.

3. Cut in butter with pastry blender or two knives until mixture resembles coarse crumbs. Add buttermilk; mix until slightly sticky dough forms. Transfer dough to prepared baking sheet; shape into 8-inch round.

4. Bake 50 to 60 minutes or until bread is golden and crust is firm. Cool on baking sheet 10 minutes; remove to wire rack to cool completely. *Makes 12 servings*

Orange-Currant Scones

1½ cups all-purpose flour
¼ cup plus 1 teaspoon sugar, divided
1 teaspoon baking powder
¼ teaspoon salt
¼ teaspoon baking soda
⅓ cup currants
1 tablespoon grated orange peel
6 tablespoons cold butter, cut into small pieces
½ cup buttermilk, plain yogurt or sour cream

1. Preheat oven to 425°F. Lightly grease baking sheet or line with parchment paper.

2. Combine flour, ¼ cup sugar, baking powder, salt and baking soda in large bowl. Stir in currants and orange peel.

3. Cut in butter with pastry blender or two knives until mixture resembles coarse crumbs. Add buttermilk; stir until mixture forms soft sticky dough that clings together.

4. Shape dough into ball; pat into 8-inch round on prepared baking sheet. Cut dough into 8 wedges with floured knife. Sprinkle with remaining 1 teaspoon sugar.

5. Bake 18 to 20 minutes or until lightly browned. Serve warm. *Makes 8 scones*

Oatmeal Honey Bread

1½ to 2 cups all-purpose flour
1 cup plus 1 tablespoon old-fashioned oats, divided
½ cup whole wheat flour
1 package (¼ ounce) rapid-rise active dry yeast
1 teaspoon salt
1⅓ cups plus 1 tablespoon water, divided
¼ cup honey
2 tablespoons butter
1 egg

1. Combine 1½ cups all-purpose flour, 1 cup oats, whole wheat flour, yeast and salt in large bowl.

2. Heat 1⅓ cups water, honey and butter in small saucepan over low heat until honey dissolves and butter melts. Let cool to 130°F (temperature of very hot tap water). Add to flour mixture; beat with electric mixer at medium speed 2 minutes. Add additional flour by tablespoonfuls until dough begins to cling together. Dough should be shaggy and very sticky, not dry. (Dough should not form a ball and/or clean side of bowl.)

3. Attach dough hook to mixer; knead at medium-low speed 4 minutes. Transfer dough to large greased bowl; turn to grease top. Cover and let rise in warm place 45 minutes or until doubled.

4. Spray 8×4-inch loaf pan with nonstick cooking spray. Punch down dough; transfer to floured work surface. Flatten and stretch dough into 8-inch-long oval. Bring long sides together and pinch to seal; fold over short ends and pinch to seal. Place in prepared pan seam side down. Cover and let rise in warm place 20 to 30 minutes or until dough reaches top of pan.

5. Preheat oven to 375°F. Beat egg and remaining 1 tablespoon water in small bowl. Brush top of loaf with egg mixture; sprinkle with remaining 1 tablespoon oats. Bake 30 to 35 minutes or until bread sounds hollow when tapped (about 190°F on instant-read thermometer). Cool on wire rack. *Makes 1 (8-inch) loaf*

Tip: To knead by hand, transfer dough to floured work surface. Begin by folding sticky dough over using dough scraper or spatula. When dough becomes more manageable, knead by hand about 6 minutes or until almost smooth. Sprinkle work surface with small amounts of flour as needed to prevent sticking, but dough should remain supple and soft.

Barm Brack

4 to 4½ cups all-purpose flour
½ cup plus 1 teaspoon sugar, divided
1 package (¼ ounce) rapid-rise active dry yeast
1 teaspoon salt
½ teaspoon ground cinnamon
¼ teaspoon ground nutmeg
¾ cup plus 1 tablespoon water, divided
¾ cup milk
¼ cup (½ stick) butter, softened
1 egg
1 cup golden raisins (optional)
½ cup chopped dried or candied fruit (apricots, cherries, prunes, etc.)

1. Place 4 cups flour in large bowl. Stir in ½ cup sugar, yeast, salt, cinnamon and nutmeg. Combine ¾ cup water, milk and butter in small saucepan; heat over low heat until butter melts and temperature reaches 120° to 130°F. Add milk mixture to flour mixture; beat with electric mixer at medium speed 2 minutes or until well blended. Beat in egg.

2. Gradually add additional flour until slightly sticky dough forms. Attach dough hook to mixer; knead at low speed 4 minutes or 8 minutes by hand on lightly floured surface. Transfer dough to large greased bowl; turn to grease top. Cover and let rise in warm place 45 minutes to 1 hour or until doubled.

3. Spray two 8×4-inch loaf pans with nonstick cooking spray. Punch down dough; transfer to floured surface. Knead in raisins, if desired, and dried fruit. Divide dough into two balls; cover and let rest 5 minutes. To shape loaves, flatten and stretch each ball of dough into oval shape. Bring long sides together and pinch to seal; fold over short ends and pinch to seal. Place in prepared pans seam side down. Cover and let rise in warm place 45 minutes or until dough almost reaches tops of pans.

4. Preheat oven to 375°F. Bake 35 to 40 minutes or until browned. (Cover loosely with foil if loaves begin to overbrown.) Dissolve remaining 1 teaspoon sugar in 1 tablespoon water in small bowl. Brush over loaves; bake 2 minutes. Cool in pans 2 minutes; remove to wire rack to cool slightly. Serve warm. *Makes 2 loaves*

Note: This fruity loaf is traditionally served on Halloween. Charms are baked into the bread to predict the future. If your piece of barm brack contains a ring, you will get married within the year; if you find a coin, you'll become rich.

Beer and Bacon Muffins

6 slices bacon, chopped
2 cups chopped onions
3 teaspoons sugar, divided
¼ teaspoon dried thyme
1½ cups all-purpose flour
¾ cup grated Parmesan cheese
2 teaspoons baking powder
½ teaspoon salt
¾ cup lager or other light-colored beer
2 eggs
¼ cup extra virgin olive oil

1. Preheat oven to 375°F. Grease 12 standard (2½-inch) muffin cups.

2. Cook bacon in large skillet over medium heat until crisp, stirring occasionally. Remove bacon to paper towel-lined plate with slotted spoon. Add onions, 1 teaspoon sugar and thyme to skillet; cook 12 minutes or until onions are golden brown, stirring occasionally. Cool 5 minutes; stir in bacon.

3. Combine flour, cheese, baking powder, salt and remaining 2 teaspoons sugar in large bowl. Whisk lager, eggs and oil in medium bowl. Add to flour mixture; stir just until moistened. Gently stir in onion mixture. Spoon batter evenly into prepared muffin cups.

4. Bake 15 minutes or until toothpick inserted into centers comes out clean. Cool in pan 5 minutes. Serve warm or at room temperature. *Makes 12 servings*

Treacle Bread (Brown Soda Bread)

2 cups all-purpose flour
1 cup whole wheat flour
1 teaspoon baking soda
½ teaspoon salt
½ teaspoon ground ginger
1¼ cups buttermilk, plus additional as needed
3 tablespoons dark molasses (preferably blackstrap)

1. Preheat oven to 375°F. Line baking sheet with parchment paper.

2. Combine all-purpose flour, whole wheat flour, baking soda, salt and ginger in large bowl; mix well. Combine buttermilk and molasses in small bowl; mix well.

3. Stir buttermilk mixture into flour mixture. Add additional buttermilk by tablespoonfuls if needed to make dry, rough dough. Transfer dough to floured surface; knead 8 to 10 times or just until smooth. (Do not overknead.) Shape dough into round loaf about 1½ inches thick. Transfer to prepared baking sheet.

4. Use floured knife to cut halfway through dough, scoring into quarters (called farls in Ireland). Sprinkle top of dough with additional flour, if desired.

5. Bake about 35 minutes or until bread sounds hollow when tapped. Remove to wire rack to cool slightly. Serve warm.

Makes 6 to 8 servings

Note: Treacle Bread can be sliced or pulled apart into farls.

Irish-Style Scones

3 eggs, divided
½ cup whipping cream
1½ teaspoons vanilla
2 cups all-purpose flour
2 teaspoons baking powder
¼ teaspoon salt
¼ cup (½ stick) cold butter
¼ cup finely chopped pitted dates
¼ cup golden raisins
1 teaspoon water
Orange marmalade
Whipped cream or crème fraîche

1. Preheat oven to 375°F. Lightly grease large baking sheet or line with parchment paper.

2. Beat 2 eggs, cream and vanilla in medium bowl until well blended. Combine flour, baking powder and salt in large bowl. Cut in butter with pastry blender or two knives until mixture resembles coarse crumbs. Stir in dates and raisins. Add cream mixture; mix just until dry ingredients are moistened.

3. Knead dough with floured hands four times on lightly floured surface. Place dough on prepared baking sheet; pat into 8-inch circle. Gently score dough into six wedges with sharp wet knife, cutting three-fourths of the way into dough. Beat remaining egg and water in small bowl; brush lightly over dough.

4. Bake 18 to 20 minutes or until golden brown. Cool 5 minutes on wire rack. Cut into wedges. Serve warm with marmalade and whipped cream. *Makes 6 scones*

DESSERTS

Apple Buttermilk Pie

2 medium Granny Smith apples
3 eggs
1½ cups sugar, divided
1 cup buttermilk
⅓ cup butter, melted
2 tablespoons all-purpose flour
2 teaspoons ground cinnamon, divided
2 teaspoons vanilla
¾ teaspoon ground nutmeg, divided
1 (9-inch) unbaked pie shell
Whipped cream and additional ground cinnamon (optional)

1. Preheat oven to 350°F. Peel and core apples; cut into small chunks. Place apples in small bowl; cover with cold water and set aside.

2. Beat eggs in medium bowl with electric mixer at low speed until blended. Add all but 1 teaspoon sugar, buttermilk, butter, flour, 1 teaspoon cinnamon, vanilla and ½ teaspoon nutmeg; beat at low speed until well blended.

3. Drain apples thoroughly; place in unbaked pie shell. Pour buttermilk mixture over apples. Combine remaining 1 teaspoon sugar, 1 teaspoon cinnamon and ¼ teaspoon nutmeg in small bowl; sprinkle over top.

4. Bake 50 to 60 minutes or until knife inserted into center comes out clean. Serve warm or at room temperature. Garnish with whipped cream and additional cinnamon. Store leftovers in refrigerator.

Makes 8 servings

Lemon Tart

1 refrigerated pie crust (half of 15-ounce package)
5 eggs
1 tablespoon cornstarch
1 cup sugar
½ cup (1 stick) unsalted butter
½ cup lemon juice

1. Position rack in center of oven. Preheat oven to 450°F.

2. Line 9-inch tart pan with pie crust, pressing to fit securely against side of pan. Trim off any excess crust. Prick bottom and side of crust with fork. Bake 9 to 10 minutes or until golden brown. Cool completely. *Reduce oven temperature to 350°F.*

3. Meanwhile, whisk eggs and cornstarch in medium bowl. Combine sugar, butter and lemon juice in small saucepan over medium-low heat; cook and stir just until butter melts. Whisk in egg mixture; cook 8 to 10 minutes or until thickened, stirring constantly. (Do not let mixture come to a boil.). Transfer to medium bowl; stir 1 minute or until cooled slightly. Let cool 10 minutes.

4. Pour cooled lemon curd into baked crust. Bake 25 to 30 minutes or until set. Cool completely before cutting. Store leftovers in refrigerator. *Makes 8 to 10 servings*

Fresh Fruit Fool

1 cup sliced peeled peaches (about 2 small)
1 cup sliced peeled plums (about 2 large)
1 cup fresh raspberries
8 tablespoons powdered sugar, divided
1 tablespoon lemon juice
1 cup whipping cream
   Grated lemon peel (optional)

1. Combine peaches, plums, raspberries, 6 tablespoons powdered sugar and lemon juice in blender; blend until smooth. Cover and refrigerate at least 1 hour or up to 24 hours.

2. Beat cream in medium bowl with electric mixer at high speed until soft peaks form. Add remaining 2 tablespoons powdered sugar; beat until stiff. Fold into fruit mixture.

3. Spoon into four serving bowls; garnish with lemon peel. *Makes 4 servings*

Pecan Bread Pudding with Caramel Whiskey Sauce

8 cups cubed egg bread or brioche (about 10 ounces)
½ cup coarsely chopped pecans, toasted*
1⅔ cups sugar, divided
3 eggs
3 egg yolks
3 cups whole milk
1 teaspoon vanilla
¼ teaspoon salt
¼ teaspoon ground nutmeg
1 teaspoon ground cinnamon
2 tablespoons butter, cut into pieces
⅓ cup whipping cream
2 to 3 tablespoons Irish whiskey or bourbon

*To toast pecans, spread in single layer on baking sheet. Bake in preheated 350°F oven 8 to 10 minutes or until lightly toasted, stirring occasionally.

1. Grease 13×9-inch baking dish or shallow 2-quart casserole. Combine bread cubes and pecans in prepared dish.

2. Beat ¾ cup sugar, eggs and egg yolks in medium bowl until blended. Add milk, vanilla, salt and nutmeg; beat until well blended. Pour egg mixture over bread mixture. Let stand 15 to 20 minutes, pressing down on bread occasionally.

3. Preheat oven to 350°F. Combine ¼ cup sugar and cinnamon in small bowl; sprinkle over bread mixture.

4. Bake 45 to 50 minutes or until puffed and golden brown. Cool on wire rack 15 minutes.

5. For sauce, place butter in small heavy saucepan. Add remaining ⅔ cup sugar; shake pan to make even layer but do not stir. Cook over medium heat 5 minutes or until golden and bubbly. Stir mixture; cook 2 minutes or until deep golden brown. Gradually stir in cream. (Mixture will sizzle.) Cook and stir until smooth. Remove from heat; stir in whiskey, 1 tablespoon at a time. Serve bread pudding warm or at room temperature topped with warm sauce.

Makes 8 servings

Tip: Sauce may be prepared up to 2 days in advance and refrigerated. Reheat the sauce just before serving.

Apricot Oatmeal Bars

1½ cups old-fashioned oats
1¼ cups all-purpose flour
 ½ cup packed brown sugar
 1 teaspoon ground ginger, divided
 ½ teaspoon salt
 ½ teaspoon baking soda
 ½ teaspoon ground cinnamon
 ¾ cup (1½ sticks) butter, melted
1¼ cups apricot preserves

1. Preheat oven to 350°F. Line 8-inch square baking pan with foil.

2. Combine oats, flour, brown sugar, ½ teaspoon ginger, salt, baking soda and cinnamon in large bowl. Add butter; stir just until moistened and crumbly. Reserve 1½ cups oat mixture. Press remaining oat mixture evenly onto bottom of prepared pan.

3. Combine preserves and remaining ½ teaspoon ginger in small bowl. Spread preserves mixture evenly over crust. Sprinkle with reserved oat mixture.

4. Bake 30 minutes or until golden brown. Cool completely in pan on wire rack. Cut into bars. *Makes 9 servings*

Poached Dried Fruit Compote

1½ cups water
 8 ounces mixed dried fruit, such as apricots, pears, apples and prunes
 ½ cup Riesling or other white wine
 2 cinnamon sticks
 4 whole cloves

1. Combine water, dried fruit, wine, cinnamon sticks and cloves in medium saucepan; bring to a boil over high heat. Reduce heat to low; simmer, uncovered, 12 to 15 minutes or until fruit is tender.

2. Cool slightly; discard cinnamon sticks and cloves. Serve warm, at room temperature or chilled. *Makes 6 servings*

Lenten Apple Cake

4 medium apples, cut into ¼-inch slices (4 cups)
Juice of ½ lemon
3 cups all-purpose flour
1 cup sugar
¾ cup chopped almonds
1½ teaspoons baking soda
1 teaspoon ground cinnamon
½ teaspoon salt
½ teaspoon ground nutmeg
1 cup vegetable oil
1 teaspoon vanilla

1. Preheat over to 350°F. Grease 13×9-inch baking pan.

2. Place apple slices in medium bowl. Drizzle with lemon juice and sprinkle with sugar; toss to coat. Let stand 20 minutes or until juice forms.

3. Combine flour, sugar, almonds, baking soda, cinnamon, salt and nutmeg in large bowl; mix well. Add oil and vanilla; stir until well blended. Stir in apple mixture. Spread batter in prepared pan.

4. Bake about 35 minutes or until browned and toothpick inserted into center comes out clean. Cool in pan on wire rack 10 minutes. Serve warm.   *Makes 16 servings*

Note: Either whole skin-on almonds or sliced almonds can be used.

Strawberry-Rhubarb Crisp

4 cups sliced rhubarb (1-inch pieces)
3 cups sliced strawberries (about 1 pint)
¾ cup granulated sugar
⅓ cup plus ¼ cup all-purpose flour, divided
1 tablespoon grated lemon peel
1 cup quick oats
½ cup packed brown sugar
1 teaspoon ground cinnamon
½ teaspoon salt
⅓ cup butter, melted

1. Preheat oven to 375°F. Combine rhubarb and strawberries in large bowl.

2. Combine granulated sugar, ¼ cup flour and lemon peel in small bowl. Sprinkle over fruit; toss to coat. Transfer to 9-inch square baking pan.

3. Combine oats, brown sugar, remaining ⅓ cup flour, cinnamon and salt in medium bowl. Stir in butter until mixture is crumbly. Sprinkle over rhubarb mixture.

4. Bake 45 to 50 minutes or until filling is bubbly and topping is lightly browned. Serve warm or at room temperature.

Makes 8 servings

Lemon Curd

6 tablespoons butter
1 cup sugar
6 tablespoons lemon juice
2 teaspoons grated lemon peel
3 eggs, lightly beaten

1. Melt butter in double boiler set over simmering water. Stir in sugar, lemon juice and lemon peel.

2. Stir in eggs until blended. Cook and stir 15 to 20 minutes or until mixture is thick and smooth. Remove from heat; let cool. (Curd will thicken as it cools.) Cover and refrigerate 2 hours or until cold. Serve chilled. Store in refrigerator up to 3 weeks.

Makes 1¾ cups

Chocolate Stout Cake

2 cups all-purpose flour
¾ cup unsweetened cocoa powder
1 teaspoon baking soda
¼ teaspoon salt
1 cup packed brown sugar
¾ cup (1½ sticks) butter, softened
½ cup granulated sugar
1 teaspoon vanilla
3 eggs
1 cup stout, at room temperature
Cream Cheese Frosting (recipe follows)

1. Preheat oven to 350°F. Grease 13×9-inch baking pan. Combine flour, cocoa, baking soda and salt in medium bowl.

2. Beat brown sugar, butter and granulated sugar in large bowl with electric mixer at medium speed until light and fluffy. Beat in vanilla. Add eggs, one at a time, beating well after each addition. Add flour mixture alternately with stout, beating until blended after each addition. Pour batter into prepared pan.

3. Bake 35 to 40 minutes or until toothpick inserted into center comes out clean. Cool completely on wire rack.

4. Prepare Cream Cheese Frosting. Spread frosting over cake. *Makes 12 servings*

Cream Cheese Frosting

1 package (8 ounces) cream cheese, softened
¼ cup (½ stick) butter, softened
4 cups powdered sugar
1 teaspoon vanilla
1 to 2 tablespoons milk

Beat cream cheese and butter in large bowl with electric mixer at medium speed until creamy. Gradually beat in powdered sugar and vanilla until smooth. Add enough milk to make spreadable frosting; beat until smooth. *Makes 2½ cups*

Bread and Butter Pudding

3 tablespoons butter, softened
1 pound egg bread or firm white bread, sliced
⅔ cup golden raisins
¾ cup sugar, divided
1 teaspoon ground cinnamon
¼ teaspoon ground nutmeg
2 cups half-and-half
2 cups whole milk
6 eggs
1½ teaspoons vanilla

1. Preheat oven to 350°F. Grease 1½-quart or 13×9-inch baking dish.

2. Lightly butter both sides of bread slices; cut into 1½-inch pieces. Combine bread and raisins in prepared baking dish. Combine ¼ cup sugar, cinnamon and nutmeg in small bowl; sprinkle over bread mixture and toss to coat.

3. Beat half-and-half, milk, eggs, remaining ½ cup sugar and vanilla in large bowl until well blended. Pour over bread mixture; let stand 10 minutes.

4. Bake about 1 hour or until pudding is set, puffed and golden brown. Serve warm or at room temperature. *Makes 8 to 10 servings*

Irish Coffee

6 ounces freshly brewed strong black coffee
2 teaspoons packed brown sugar
2 ounces Irish whiskey
¼ cup whipping cream

Combine coffee and brown sugar in Irish coffee glass or mug. Stir in whiskey. Pour cream over back of spoon into coffee. *Makes 1 serving*

Gingerbread with Lemon Sauce

2½ cups all-purpose flour
1½ teaspoons ground cinnamon
1 teaspoon ground ginger
½ teaspoon baking soda
½ teaspoon salt
½ cup (1 stick) butter, softened
¾ cup packed brown sugar
⅓ cup light molasses
1 egg
¾ cup stout, at room temperature
Lemon Sauce (recipe follows)
Grated lemon peel (optional)

1. Preheat oven to 350°F. Grease bottom of 9-inch square baking pan. Combine flour, cinnamon, ginger, baking soda and salt in medium bowl.

2. Beat butter and brown sugar in large bowl with electric mixer at medium speed until light and fluffy. Add molasses and egg; beat until well blended. Add flour mixture alternately with stout, beating until blended after each addition. Pour batter into prepared pan.

3. Bake 35 to 40 minutes or until toothpick inserted in center comes out clean. Cool completely in pan on wire rack. Prepare Lemon Sauce.

4. Cut cake into squares. Top with sauce and lemon peel, if desired.   *Makes 9 servings*

Lemon Sauce

1 cup granulated sugar
¾ cup whipping cream
½ cup (1 stick) butter
1 tablespoon lemon juice
2 teaspoons grated lemon peel

Combine granulated sugar, cream and butter in small saucepan; cook and stir over medium heat until butter is melted. Reduce heat to low; simmer 5 minutes. Stir in lemon juice and lemon peel. Cool slightly.

Apple Blackberry Crisp

4 cups sliced apples
Juice of ½ lemon
2 tablespoons granulated sugar
2 tablespoons Irish cream liqueur
1 teaspoon ground cinnamon, divided
1 cup old-fashioned oats
6 tablespoons cold butter, cut into pieces
⅔ cup packed brown sugar
¼ cup all-purpose flour
1 cup blackberries
Irish Whipped Cream (optional, recipe follows)

1. Preheat oven to 375°F. Grease 9-inch oval or 8-inch square baking dish.

2. Place apples in large bowl; drizzle with lemon juice. Stir in granulated sugar, liqueur and ½ teaspoon cinnamon.

3. For topping, combine oats, butter, brown sugar, flour and remaining ½ teaspoon cinnamon in food processor; pulse until mixture is combined, leaving some some chunks remaining.

4. Gently stir blackberries into apple mixture. Transfer to prepared baking dish. Sprinkle with topping.

5. Bake 30 to 40 minutes or until bubbly. Serve with Irish Whipped Cream, if desired.

Makes 6 servings

Irish Whipped Cream: Beat 1 cup heavy whipping cream and 2 tablespoons Irish cream liqueur in large bowl with electric mixer at high speed until slightly thickened. Add 1 to 2 tablespoons powdered sugar; beat until soft peaks form.

Tip: This crisp can also be made without the blackberries; just add an additional 1 cup of sliced apples.

Ginger Stout Cake

2 cups all-purpose flour

2 teaspoons ground ginger

1½ teaspoons baking powder

1½ teaspoons baking soda

¾ teaspoon ground cinnamon

½ teaspoon salt

¼ teaspoon ground cloves

½ cup (1 stick) butter, softened

1 tablespoon grated fresh ginger *or* 1 teaspoon ground ginger

1 cup granulated sugar

½ cup packed brown sugar

3 eggs

1 bottle (11 ounces) Irish stout

½ cup molasses

Whipped cream and additional ground cinnamon (optional)

1. Preheat oven to 350°F. Grease 13×9-inch baking pan. Combine flour, ground ginger, baking powder, baking soda, cinnamon, salt and cloves in medium bowl.

2. Beat butter and grated ginger in large bowl with electric mixer at medium speed until creamy. Add granulated sugar and brown sugar; beat until light and fluffy Add eggs, one at a time, beating well after each addition.

3. Combine stout and molasses in small bowl. Alternately add flour mixture and stout mixture to butter mixture, beating well after each addition. Pour batter into prepared pan.

4. Bake 45 minutes or until toothpick inserted into center comes out clean. Cool completely in pan on wire rack. Garnish with whipped cream and additional cinnamon.

Makes 12 to 15 servings

Molded Shortbread

1½ cups all-purpose flour
¼ teaspoon salt
¾ cup (1½ sticks) butter, softened
⅓ cup sugar
1 egg

1. Preheat oven to temperature recommended by shortbread mold manufacturer. Grease 10-inch ceramic shortbread mold.

2. Combine flour and salt in medium bowl. Beat butter and sugar in large bowl with electric mixer at medium speed until light and fluffy. Add egg; beat until well blended. Gradually add flour mixture; beat at low speed until well blended.

3. Press dough firmly into mold. Bake, cool and remove from mold according to manufacturer's directions.   *Makes 1 shortbread mold*

Note: If shortbread mold is not available, preheat oven to 350°F. Shape dough into 1-inch balls. Place 2 inches apart on ungreased cookie sheets; press with fork to flatten. Bake 18 to 20 minutes or until edges are lightly browned. Cool cookies on cookie sheets 2 minutes; remove to wire racks to cool completely. Makes 2 dozen cookies.

Rhubarb Tart

1 refrigerated pie crust (half of 15-ounce package)
4 cups sliced rhubarb (½-inch pieces)
1¼ cups sugar
¼ cup all-purpose flour
2 tablespoons butter, cut into small pieces
¼ cup old-fashioned oats

1. Preheat oven to 450°F. Line 9-inch pie plate with pie crust. Trim excess crust; flute or crimp edge.

2. Combine rhubarb, sugar and flour in medium bowl; mix well. Place mixture in prepared crust. Top with butter; sprinkle with oats.

3. Bake 10 minutes. *Reduce oven temperature to 350°F.* Bake 40 minutes or until crust is golden brown and filling is bubbly.   *Makes 8 servings*

VOLUME MEASUREMENTS (dry)

1/8 teaspoon = 0.5 mL
1/4 teaspoon = 1 mL
1/2 teaspoon = 2 mL
3/4 teaspoon = 4 mL
1 teaspoon = 5 mL
1 tablespoon = 15 mL
2 tablespoons = 30 mL
1/4 cup = 60 mL
1/3 cup = 75 mL
1/2 cup = 125 mL
2/3 cup = 150 mL
3/4 cup = 175 mL
1 cup = 250 mL
2 cups = 1 pint = 500 mL
3 cups = 750 mL
4 cups = 1 quart = 1 L

VOLUME MEASUREMENTS (fluid)

1 fluid ounce (2 tablespoons) = 30 mL
4 fluid ounces (1/2 cup) = 125 mL
8 fluid ounces (1 cup) = 250 mL
12 fluid ounces (1 1/2 cups) = 375 mL
16 fluid ounces (2 cups) = 500 mL

WEIGHTS (mass)

1/2 ounce = 15 g
1 ounce = 30 g
3 ounces = 90 g
4 ounces = 120 g
8 ounces = 225 g
10 ounces = 285 g
12 ounces = 360 g
16 ounces = 1 pound = 450 g

DIMENSIONS

1/16 inch = 2 mm
1/8 inch = 3 mm
1/4 inch = 6 mm
1/2 inch = 1.5 cm
3/4 inch = 2 cm
1 inch = 2.5 cm

OVEN TEMPERATURES

250°F = 120°C
275°F = 140°C
300°F = 150°C
325°F = 160°C
350°F = 180°C
375°F = 190°C
400°F = 200°C
425°F = 220°C
450°F = 230°C

BAKING PAN SIZES

Utensil	Size in Inches/Quarts	Metric Volume	Size in Centimeters
Baking or Cake Pan (square or rectangular)	8×8×2	2 L	20×20×5
	9×9×2	2.5 L	23×23×5
	12×8×2	3 L	30×20×5
	13×9×2	3.5 L	33×23×5
Loaf Pan	8×4×3	1.5 L	20×10×7
	9×5×3	2 L	23×13×7
Round Layer Cake Pan	8×1½	1.2 L	20×4
	9×1½	1.5 L	23×4
Pie Plate	8×1¼	750 mL	20×3
	9×1¼	1 L	23×3
Baking Dish or Casserole	1 quart	1 L	—
	1½ quart	1.5 L	—
	2 quart	2 L	—